SEX LIVES
OF THE KINGS
&
QUEENS OF
ENGLAND

Journalist and author, Nigel Cawthorne has had his work
published on both sides of the Atlantic. He has written many
books on subjects as diverse as computing, politics, finance, sex
and American football. He has contributed to many newspapers,
including: *The Financial Times, The News of the World, The Daily Mail,
The New York Herald-Tribune.*

In the same series by Nigel Cawthorne:

Sex Lives of the Popes
Sex Lives of the U.S. Presidents
Sex Lives of the Great Dictators

All published by Prion.

SEX LIVES
OF THE KINGS
&
QUEENS OF
ENGLAND

An irreverent exposé of the Monarchs
from Henry VIII to the present day

Nigel Cawthorne

PRION

First published in Great Britain in 1994
Revised paperback edition published 1996
This revised edition published 2004 by

Prion
an imprint of the
Carlton Publishing Group
20 Mortimer Street
London W1T 3JW

A catalogue record for this book is available from the
British Library

ISBN 1 85375 536 2

Printed in Great Britain
by Mackays

CONTENTS

INTRODUCTION

Recently, much criticism has been levelled at the press for intruding on the private lives of the royal family. But there is nothing new about this. People have always been fascinated by the sexual behaviour of kings and queens, princes and princesses. In its most innocent guise, this interest is the stuff of fairytales. A more explicit form manifests itself in ancient ballads, pamphlets and scandal sheets. Today, the tabloids provide the most common outlet.

But there is more to this fascination with royal sexual antics than mere prurience. Throughout history the sleeping partners of a reigning monarch could be a matter of life or death. Political alliances were often based on royal marriages, so the success of a marital relationship could vitally affect both the foreign policy and the welfare of the country. The siring of an heir to the throne could make the difference between a period of political stability and a civil war. From the time of

1

James II up to the birth of Princess Margaret, at least one member of the government – and sometimes the entire Privy Council, along with the Archbishop of Canterbury and other dignitaries – had to witness the birth of a royal child. This was to establish beyond doubt the maternity of the new heir. Questions over a royal child's paternity could lead to a political intrigue or war.

The sexual incompatibility of a royal couple could turn a united court and government into warring factions. Sexual infidelity has led to cabals and conspiracies. Royal divorces have created huge upheavals and royal mistresses have often been cultivated by political parties and foreign powers for their influence between the sheets. Willing sexual partners with particular charms or talents have often been introduced into the monarch's circle by those seeking political power.

Even though the British royal family no longer enjoys the power it once did, the sexual behaviour of its members is still of legitimate interest to the nation. Gross sexual misconduct by any of them could seriously undermine the position of the monarchy.

In particular, marital problems between the Prince and Princess of Wales could have devastating political consequences. As it is, Diana had to be certified a virgin before she could marry the heir to the throne. If she has lovers, both she and her paramours are technically committing treason.

The Queen is the head of the Church of England, which does not condone any sort of sexual impropriety. Charles will inherit this position and, as first family, the royals should be above reproach. They are the very symbol of our country; their sexual behaviour reflects on us all. So it is valid to ask what sort of family they are.

Occupying centre stage, monarchs have always had more sexual opportunities than the rest of us. They have power, which – as Henry Kissinger once remarked – is the ultimate aphrodisiac. Traditionally, we allow our rulers certain sexual privileges. Commoners are usually eager to submit themselves to the monarch's whims. Husbands and wives often consent – and even collude – when their spouse is involved with a royal. George Keppel, for example, thought that it was his patriotic duty to accommodate his wife's affair with Edward VII. He felt honoured by it and was genuinely upset when the King died.

There is certainly nothing unique about the behaviour of the British royal family. Monarchs the world over – as well as those in ancient and in primitive cultures – have conducted themselves equally badly. Catherine the Great of Russia, the kings of Bavaria and the emperors of ancient Rome were fabled for their excesses – though the tale that Catherine the Great died during a sex act with a horse, crushed when the crane supporting the poor animal broke, is probably apocryphal. Cleopatra was a victim of her own sexual allure, while Solomon, according to the Book of Kings, 'loved many strange women'. The emperors of China and Arabian potentates once boasted hundreds of concubines. Even today, the current King of Lesotho has several hundred wives to satisfy. How does he cope?

But are these royal sexual appetites the result of normal healthy desires given full rein by the monarchy's unlimited power? Or do they stem from the public's expectations?

Some figures of authority seem to revel in the sexual subjugation of their underlings. They govern by dominating those closest to the seat of power, by seducing them or their wives, or else by instigating impossibly high codes of morality in order to deny them sex. The Reverend Jim Jones and Charles Manson both used sex to inspire such loyalty in their followers that they were willing to commit suicide or murder upon command. In *The Naked Ape*, zoologist Desmond Morris also pointed out that, in colonies of apes, powerful individuals maintain their position by sexually subjugating the weaker ones.

The indiscretions of the royal family were the very basis of the scandal sheets, which were the forerunners of today's newspapers. But although readers have always craved this titillating diet, modern newspapers have often turned a blind eye to the royals' sexual excesses.

The behaviour of the present royal family – and the current media reaction towards it – cannot simply be judged by contemporary standards. It must be seen in the broad historical context of the dynasties which have ruled over us for centuries. After all, it is by tracing their lineage back through the ancient kings and queens of Britain, France and Germany that the present royal family claim their right to reign over us.

Back in the mists of legend, the peace of King Arthur's fabled Camelot was shattered when Lancelot stole the affections of Guinevere. Arthur himself was killed by the son of his incestuous union with his sister, the enchantress Morgan le Fay, and the country was in turmoil for centuries afterwards.

Although subsequent kings, by and large, avoided incest, most fathered illegitimate offspring. These were useful as loyal lieutenants and as marriage fodder for cementing alliances. King Ida, who reigned from 547 to 599, sired twelve bastard sons. Ethelfrith, 592–616, had five and Oswiu, 641–670, just one; illegitimate daughters, in those days, were not counted.

In 746, King Ethelbald of Mercia was rebuked by St Boniface for being 'governed by lust'. Undaunted by this admonition, Ethelbald, 858–860, King of the West Saxons, married his own stepmother to maintain the alliance his father had forged with the King of the Franks. The second consort of King Edgar, 959–975, was in fact his mistress, though their son still inherited the crown. In 786, it had been recommended that all children 'begotten by adultery or incest' should be allowed to succeed to the throne.

Ethelred the Unready, king from 978 to 1016, was the illegitimate son of the concubine Aelgifu, who is supposed to have given birth to at least two more kings. There may be some confusion here because one of them, King Canute, 1016–1035, also had a mistress called Aelgifu. But this was not necessarily the same woman as his father's and grandfather's mistress – though such things do happen in royal circles. Canute's son, Harold Harefoot, 1037–1040, also had a mistress with the same name, but that was clearly just a coincidence. Things were very different in those days, though. St Jerome was acknowledging the prevalence of adultery when he declared: 'Nothing is more vile than to love a wife like a mistress.'

The Norman Conquest in 1066 was a direct result of irregular sexual habits. Edward the Confessor was such a pious man that he practised chastity – even within marriage. This bought him canonisation and a frustrated wife, but it also created a power vacuum. When he died, Harold of Wessex seized the throne. But William, Duke of Normandy – or William the Bastard as he is known in France – opposed him. William's father, Robert of Normandy, a bisexual, had sired him after abducting a peasant girl called Heleve, whom he had spotted washing her clothes in a stream. He took her back to his castle, where he held her captive and fathered two children by her. After her release, Heleve went on to make a rather advantageous match with Baron Heliun, Vicomte of Conteville.

When Robert died he left no legitimate heir. The Dukes of Normandy would not accept the bastard William and he spent most of his early life fighting for his birthright. So by 1066, when he came up against Harold at the Battle of Hastings, William was a seasoned campaigner.

Henry I was notorious for his mistresses. He had over twenty illegitimate children. His only legitimate son, William, was drowned trying to save his illegitimate half-sister Maud. Another illegitimate half-sister Matilda took the throne, but spent her reign fighting a civil war against Stephen, one of William the Conqueror's grandsons.

Henry II married Eleanor of Aquitaine. She had been married to Louis VII, but grew jealous when she discovered that, during his excursions to the crusades, his love for his fellow knights was not always platonic (though she herself was said to have bestowed her favours on her uncle, Raimond of Poitou, while Louis was away.) Eventually, she had her marriage annulled and married Henry of Anjou, the future Henry II. The marriage eventually broke down when Henry embarked on an affair with 'Fair Rosamund'.

The Order of the Garter was supposed to have been started by Edward III, when the Countess of Salisbury lost her garter while dancing. To spare her blushes, he picked it up, saying 'Honi soit qui mal y pense' – 'Evil be to he who evil thinks.' In his old age, Edward took a mistress, Alice Perrers, a tiler's daughter from Essex. She took advantage of his premature senility and amassed more wealth than the Queen. An outraged parliament banished her from the realm, but she slipped back into the country in time to throw herself weepingly on Edward's corpse and prise the rings from his fingers.

Although married twice, Richard II was a homosexual. The extravagance of his court led to the Peasants' Revolt. Even so, he was considerate enough to legitimize the bastards of John of Gaunt, Duke of Lancaster. Some of the court refused to accept this and the ensuing dispute was a key factor in the outbreak of the War of the Roses.

Henry IV, the 'usurper', was a notorious lecher. It was said that 'no woman was there anywhere ... but he would importunely pursue his appetite and have her.' His son, the great warrior Henry V, also 'fervently followed the service of Venus as well as of Mars'.

Henry VI was more prudish. On one occasion, when a troupe of half-naked dancing girls was laid on to entertain him, Henry ran from the room crying: 'Fy, fy, for shame.' He himself was impotent. When his wife Margaret of Anjou announced that she was pregnant, he collapsed. Court gossip had it that the child was the

bastard of the Duke of Somerset and the scandal surrounding this helped Edward IV to seize the throne.

Edward was 'licentious in the extreme' according to
contemporary reports. It was said that he had been
'most insolent' to numerous women after he had seduced them. Once he grew weary of them, he simply
handed them on to his courtiers, much against their
will. 'He pursued with no discrimination the married
and the unmarried, the noble and the lowly,' it was
reported; 'however, he took none by force. He overcame all by money and promises, and having conquered
them he dismissed them.'

Be that as it may, he did threaten them. He tried to
rape the widowed Elizabeth Woodville at knifepoint.
Only when she said that she would rather die than have
him, did he promise to marry her.

1

HAL THE HORNY

Henry VIII is usually seen as the archetypal lusty monarch. Although a monstrous tyrant, his sexual excesses seem to have endeared him to the English down the ages. However, he was not the sexual athlete that his reputation suggests. It is said that he is the only British king to have had more wives than mistresses.

Despite the notoriety he earned later, Henry VIII was brought up chastely by his stern father Henry VII, away from the worldly temptations open to most young princes. He came to the throne in 1509, when he was eighteen and still unwed. Less than two months later, he married Catherine of Aragon the widow of his brother, Arthur, Prince of Wales, who had died in 1502. Although this could be seen as a cynical means of maintaining England's important alliance with Spain, Henry seems to have genuinely loved Catherine, who was six years his senior. They wrote music together, sang to one another, and went hunting and hawking in each other's company. The Grooms of the Bedchamber, who lit the King's way with torches to the Queen's bedchamber, recorded that he took the conjugal route with great regularity. For five years, he seems to have kept exclusively to her bed, fathering one son who died at two months, a daughter Mary and a number of stillborn children.

In 1514, Catherine was pregnant yet again. In accordance with the custom of the time, the royal couple did not make love during pregnancy and Henry's amorous attentions turned to Lady Anne Hastings, wife of the courtier, Sir George Hastings, and sister of the Duke of Buckingham. At this stage, Henry was not terribly adept at the intrigues of infidelity. He used one of the Grooms of the King's Bedchamber, Sir Henry Compton, to carry messages to her. Compton seized the opportunity to seduce Lady Hastings himself. One of the Queen's ladies-in-waiting, Anne's sister-in-law Elizabeth Hastings, heard of the liaison and told Sir George. He burst into his wife's chamber to find her alone with Compton, who claimed that he was not making advances to her on his own behalf. It was for the King's benefit. Soon, news of the King's amorous intentions reached the ears of the Spanish ambassador and the Queen herself.

Sir George packed his wife off to a convent and Henry vented his wrath on the court scandalmongers. The Duke of Buckingham was expelled from the royal household, along with Elizabeth Hastings. Henry would have removed more of his courtiers, according to the Spanish ambassador, had it not seemed likely that this would have inflamed the situation still further.

The Queen remained vexed with Henry over the incident and, as a result, he began to cast his eye over a number of other young mistresses. Among those who received royal attention was the Flemish-born Jane Popincourt. She was the mistress of the Duc de Longueville, a French noble held hostage in the royal household during the early years of Henry's reign. Jane's reputation as a voracious temptress was widely known. When she was named as one of the maids-of-honour in the retinue of the King's sister Mary, who was on her way to France to marry Louis XII, the latter struck her name from the list. He said that he would rather see Popincourt burned at the stake than attend his innocent bride. When Henry eventually grew tired of her as a mistress, he gave her £100 to travel to France where she was reunited with her lover de Longueville.

In 1518, Henry transferred his affections to eighteen-year old Elizabeth 'Bessie' Blount. One of the eleven children of a Shropshire knight, Bessie was a court beauty, and a star of the masques – a novel form of entertainment which blended elements of song, dance, theatre and fancy dress, and which was popular throughout the courts of Renaissance Europe. Bessie was just thirteen when she first partnered Henry in a masque at a time when he was still being faithful to his wife. In fact, Catherine was so taken with the ravishing young girl that she had them repeat their performance in her bedchamber by torchlight.

Five years later, though, their performance was not so chaste and, in the summer of 1519, Bessie presented the King with the one thing his wife could never give him: a healthy, living son. Under the circumstances, there was only one course of action Henry could take. He married her off to one of the wards of the Chancery. The child, Henry Fitzroy, was brought up as the son of Gilbert

Talboys at Rokeby Manor in Warwickshire, which Henry had provided as a dowry.

Increasingly frustrated at Catherine's inability to produce a male heir, the King briefly considered marrying Henry Fitzroy off to his half-sister Mary, the legitimate heir, so that the two could rule England jointly. But Henry died of tuberculosis in his teens, thwarting this incestuous plan.

Henry had another illegitimate child by Anne Boleyn's sister, Mary. The two young women had been sent to France where, as maids of honour to the Queen, they were to learn the ways of the French court. This was a notoriously bawdy place. One French prince had a goblet made with a picture of a couple copulating engraved on the inside. He gave this to female companions to drink from, so that he could watch their reactions as the erotic scene gradually revealed itself. Another courtier, the cleric Buraud, once apologized to a lady for only having made love a dozen times that night. He cited the medication he had been prescribed as the cause of his flagging prowess.

Mary, it seems, was eager to follow such examples. She was so promiscuous that the King, François I, who had himself been described as 'clothed in women', dubbed her a 'hackney' – medieval slang for a whore. Similarly, one Italian observer called her 'una grandissima ribald et infame sopre tutte' – 'a great prostitute and more infamous than anyone'.

Despite this dubious reputation, Mary returned to England to marry a gentleman of the privy chamber, William Carey, and later became a lady-in-waiting to Catherine of Aragon. Henry quickly took her as his mistress and their affair lasted for about two years.

Henry never acknowledged her children as his own, and Carey earned a knighthood for his compliance. A new vessel in the navy was named the *Mary Boleyn*, but there were no financial rewards and Mary found herself destitute after Henry grew tired of her.

Mary's father, the ambitious Thomas Boleyn, sought to keep in favour with the King by replacing Mary with her younger sister Anne. There were even suggestions that he had offered his wife, as well as his two daughters, but that Henry had declined, saying: 'Never with the mother.'

In contrast to France, England recognised no *maîtresse en titre* – an official mistress who ranked alongside the Queen and Anne was determined not to share the shabby treatment that the King had meted out to her older sister. When she returned from France, it was with the intention of marrying James Butler.

Anne made her debut at court in a masque entitled 'The Assault on the Castle of Virtue', which was staged at York Place, the London home of Cardinal Wolsey. Resplendent in a satin dress, Anne was one of the eight ladies chosen to represent female Virtue. They defended a castle that was assaulted by Desire, in the person of eight masked gentlemen. After several minutes of mock combat, during which the assailants were pelted with fruit and rose-water, Virtue succumbed and the ladies danced with their suitors, who then unmasked themselves. The leader of Desire's team, of course, turned out to be none other than the King.

To ward off the King's attention, Anne took up with a married man, the poet Sir Thomas Wyatt. Sir Henry Percy, the heir to the earldom of Northumberland, also proposed to her, but, aware that Henry had his eye on her, Cardinal Wolsey stepped in to prevent the match. Around this time, as his infatuation with Anne became irresistible, Henry stopped sleeping with his wife.

Even though she had been robbed of an advantageous marriage, Anne refused to become the King's mistress. Henry persisted. In a series of passionate love letters, he begged her 'to give yourself body and heart to me', even promising to 'take you for my sole mistress, rejecting all others.' He wrote longingly about the evenings he would spend in his sweetheart's arms and the kisses she would grant him. He even eulogized her 'sweet duckies [breasts] I trust soon to kiss.' But still Anne refused him.

Strangely, Anne was no great beauty. According to a Venetian diplomat, she was plain, 'of middling stature, swarthy complexion, long neck, wide mouth and bosom not much raised'. Referring to her sex appeal, he added that she 'has nothing but the King's appetite and her eyes which are black'. This was enough to enthral Henry and hold the attention of the court. The ladies aped her style. Long, hanging sleeves, which Anne wore to hide her embryonic sixth finger, and embroidered chokers, which she wore to hide a huge unsightly mole on her neck, became the fashion.

Henry rationalised his lust for the intractable Anne by arguing that his marriage to Catherine had never been legal. It was true that, as she had been married to his own elder brother, Prince Arthur, the union with Henry would normally have been forbidden by the Catholic Church. But Catherine had gained a papal dispensation after Arthur's death, by swearing that the marriage had never been consummated and that she had come to

14

Henry as a virgin. Henry now contended that this was a lie.

The Dowager Duchess of Norfolk was persuaded to testify that Catherine had indeed slept with Prince Arthur. This sin of incest, Henry argued, had blighted their union. That was why it had produced no male heirs. If he could only divorce Catherine and marry Anne, there would be a son to secure the succession.

Unfortunately, the Pope did not see it that way, largely because, at the time, he was being held hostage by Catherine's nephew, Charles V. Moreover, when Cardinal Wolsey's attempts to obtain an annulment failed, Anne, who still resented the way in which he had prevented her marriage to Sir Henry Percy, demanded Wolsey's dismissal.

Still the divorce dragged on. Finally, in 1532, six years after Henry had fallen hopelessly in love with her and ten years after he had first set eyes on her, Anne succumbed.

By mid-January 1533, she was pregnant. The prospect of a male heir spurred Henry into action and events proceeded rapidly. On 25th January, Anne and Henry were secretly married; on 23rd May, a special Act of Parliament declared his marriage to Catherine of Aragon null and void; at Whitsun, Anne was crowned Queen, and in September she gave birth – to a daughter, Elizabeth.

Perhaps it was the disappointment of the child not being a son. Perhaps it was that the consummation, after so many years of extended foreplay, came as a massive anticlimax. Perhaps it was simply that Anne was not as accomplished in bed as her sister, the insatiable Mary.

Whatever the reason, Henry soon grew tired of his new queen.

She, for her part, was not satisfied with the King's performance either. She complained to her sister-in-law, Lady Rochford, that he possessed neither skill nor virility. Despite this, Henry continued to sleep with her and she became pregnant three more times, only to miscarry on each occasion. The King, meanwhile, had no scruples about taking on a string of other lovers, to stimulate his flagging appetite.

Anne blamed one of her miscarriages on Henry's dalliance with 'another very beautiful maid.' In an attempt to oust this rival, Anne turned for advice to her lady of the bedchamber, the sly Lady Rochford. When the King discovered their plotting, the latter was immediately banished from court.

In desperation, Anne tried to interest Henry in her own cousin, Madge Shelton. But when Henry discovered that his wife was trying to manipulate his love life, he also dismissed Madge from the court – after having bedded her, of course.

By now Henry was suffering from bouts of impotence. He complained to his doctors: 'I am forty-one years old, at which age the list of man is not so quick as in lusty youth.' Even so, Anne became pregnant again in 1535. Henry was pleased, but his approval did not stop him from turning his attentions to one of Anne's maids-of-honour, the young and lovely Jane Seymour.

Then in January 1536, Catherine of Aragon died. Henry staged a tournament to mark the occasion. Henry himself took part in the jousting and was thrown from his horse. For more than two hours he lay unconscious; Anne suddenly realized how fragile her position was. If the King died, England would be thrown into civil war over the succession and she would be in great danger. This sudden attack of anxiety sent her into premature labour and she gave birth to a son – dead.

There were rumours that the foetus was deformed – a sure sign of witchcraft. Henry denied paternity and announced that the deformed foetus showed that his second marriage, too, was cursed by incest. After all, Henry had been a lover of Anne's sister before their marriage.

With Catherine dead, Anne now found herself in a highly exposed position. It would be a simple matter for the King to declare that his first marriage had been valid after all, to end his dispute with the Catholic Church, annul his marriage to Anne, and find himself yet another new wife.

To add to her difficulties, Anne was not at all popular at court. Those who had supported Catherine and were still, secretly, faithful to the Catholic Church called her 'the concubine' and 'the goggle-eyed whore'. To console herself, she began to flirt. Instantly, her enemies spread the rumour that she was taking lovers. Henry heard of these alleged infidelities and raised the boast that she had slept with a hundred men. 'You never saw a Prince, nor man, who made a greater show of his [cuckold's] horns,' one courtier wrote.

Henry's purpose was soon clear. On 2nd May 1536, Anne was arrested for adultery, incest and intent to murder the King. Four of her supposed lovers – a gentleman of the privy chamber, Sir Henry Norris, two grooms, Sir Francis Weston and William Brereton, and a handsome young musician, Mark Smeaton – along with Anne's own brother, Lord Rochford, were all arrested.

Three of them denied the charges, but Smeaton confessed to adultery with the Queen under torture.

Norris, Weston, Brereton and Smeaton were tried together and found guilty of treason. Little evidence was presented against them and no defence was permitted. They were hanged at Tyburn, cut down whilst still alive, castrated, disembowelled and, finally, had their limbs cut off.

Anne and Rochford were tried in the Great Hall of the Tower of London. Some of Anne's maids gave their accounts of the 'pastimes of the Queen's chamber', but the chief accuser was Lady Rochford who claimed that there had been 'undue familiarity' between brother and sister. Lord Rochford, his own sister alleged, had 'always been about his sister's room' and the suggestion was made that, as Henry had proved incapable of producing the male child he craved, Anne was trying to conceive one with other lovers, among them her own brother.

As evidence of incest, this was patently absurd, but there was no challenging the King's will. The judge, Anne's own uncle the Duke of Norfolk, shed a tear when he delivered the verdict, knowing that there was no alternative but to find them guilty. The sentence was mandatory. They were to be either burned or beheaded, at the King's pleasure.

Henry showed some mercy, granting his victims a swift end. Rochford faced the axe on Tower Hill and Henry paid £24 to bring an expert swordsman over from Calais to dispatch his former love on Tower Green – but not before he had divorced her. Two days before Anne's execution, the marriage was annulled on the grounds that she had previously been contracted to marry Sir Henry Percy. Although this technically nullified the charge of adultery, no one dared to mention the fact to Henry.

As Anne was preparing to die, Henry embarked on a frantic round of parties, chasing any lady he found remotely attractive. He compared his delight in this new-found freedom to the feeling a man gets when disposing of 'a thin old vicious hack in the hope of getting soon a fine horse to ride'.

The King did not take long to find his new mount. On 30th May 1536, just eleven days after the death of Anne Boleyn, he married Jane Seymour.

Henry's union with Jane was also technically incestuous, as they were cousins. However, Thomas Cranmer, the ever compliant Archbishop of Canterbury, instantly granted them a dispensation.

The daughter of a country gentleman, Jane was both modest and pious. Even though she had been at Henry's debauched court for several years, she was still reputed to be a virgin. One diplomat quipped: 'You may imagine whether being an Englishwoman and having been long at court, she would not hold it a sin to be a maid.'

Once Queen, Jane imposed her modest demeanour on others. She forbade Anne Basset to wear 'French apparel' and also demanded that she should use 'chests' – material designed to cover up plunging necklines.

At the time of Jane's wedding, the rumour spread that 'there was no fear of the occurrence of any issue of either sex.' In other words Henry was impotent. None the less, something about the girl must have inspired him, for, in February 1537, it was announced that she was pregnant. Finally, on 12th October 1537, she gave birth to Henry's long-awaited son, Edward. There were riotous celebrations. Sadly, though, the difficult labour proved too much for the delicate young woman. Jane died twelve days later.

Henry was heartbroken. Even so, he soon recovered and began to crave once more the pleasures of wifely companionship. He was also eager to sire a Duke of York, a younger brother for Edward who was a sickly child. Henry was now 48, but he remained convinced that the succession would not be properly secured until he had at least two sons. There was a problem, however, as without a queen in the court, there was no need for ladies-in-waiting and maids-of-honour. So, most of the eligible young girls were at home in the country.

John Hutton, the ambassador to the Netherlands, was charged with drawing up a list of potential mates. His roster ranged from a fourteen-year-old girl, a lady-in-waiting to the Queen of France, to a well-preserved forty-year-old widow. Hutton's principal recommendation was the sixteen-year-old Duchess Christina of Milan – an 'excellent beauty' with a 'good personage of body'. She had been married at thirteen to the Duke of Milan and widowed, without children, a year later. She was also the great niece of Catherine of Aragon.

Christina certainly excited Henry's interest, but he wanted to know more about the current crop of French princesses. He suggested a beauty pageant of five girls in Calais, but the French ambassador replied bluntly that, if the girls were to be paraded like ponies, perhaps the King would like to go further – mount them one after the other so he could pick out the best ride. Henry laughed, blushed and the idea was dropped.

The artist Hans Holbein was despatched to paint the portrait of the Duchess Christina. When Henry saw it, he was enraptured and called for musicians and masques in preparation for a wedding. However, the Lord Chamberlain, Thomas Cromwell, was keen to steer the King away from this choice. The Pope had united France and Spain against England, so the situation called for a German alliance, to restore the balance of power. Accordingly, Holbein was sent off again, to paint the portrait of Anne of Cleves.

When the English envoys arrived in Cleves, Anne and her sister Amelia were so well covered that neither their figures nor their faces could be seen. When protests were raised, the Chancellor of Cleves said: 'Why, would you see them naked?'

Holbein had to paint his portrait under the scrutiny of the Court of Cleves and erred on the side of flattery. When Henry saw the picture, he was not displeased and the details of the alliance were swiftly hammered out. The King, it was noted, was getting very 'lusty'.

Despite his gouty leg, the King rode from Greenwich to Rochester, eager to greet his new bride. As soon as he set eyes on her he was appalled. She was not the beauty that her portrait had suggested and he contemptuously described her as the 'Flanders Mare'. Her inability to speak English made matters worse, and that she appeared bored as they went through the rituals of making love. Lord Russell said he had never seen 'His Highness so marvellously astonished and abashed as on that occasion'. Henry was not one to mince words. 'I like her not,' he told Cromwell. Despite this, he bowed to the political exigencies of the situation and the marriage went ahead. Even though his wife was half his age, she excited no passion in him. On the morning after the wedding, Cromwell asked the King how the Queen was in bed.

Henry replied: 'I liked her before not well, but now I like her much worse.'

His main complaint was that she was 'not as she was reported.' Her breasts were slack and drooping, and other parts of her body were 'in such sort that (one) somewhat suspected her virginity.' Her figure was so 'disordered and indisposed' that it could not 'excite or provoke any lust in him,' and 'he could never in her company be provoked and steered to know her carnally.'

Eight days after the wedding, Henry visited his doctors. He complained that, even though he had slept with his wife each night, she was 'still as good a maid ... as ever her mother bore her.' His own virility was not in question, he protested, as he had made a number of nocturnal emissions during this period. Tactfully, the physicians urged Henry not to force himself in case he made things worse.

Anne of Cleves, meanwhile, was blissfully unaware of the problem. 'When he comes to bed, he kisses me and taketh me by the hand and biddeth me "Farewell, darling." Is not this enough?' she told Lady Rutland. The latter quietly explained that more was required from her if England was to have its Duke of York. But any discussion of the more intimate workings of the bedroom was out of the question. Anne of Cleves regarded all such matters as shameful.

The subject seemed even more humiliating when Anne and Lady Rutland were forced to repeat their conversations to a convocation of clerics, set up to investigate the validity of the marriage. Since the union had first been proposed the situation in Europe had changed. An alliance with the German states was no longer crucial. And, being a Lutheran, Anne was not popular among the Anglo-Catholics of England. To complicate matters still further, Henry now had his eye on a new lover, Anne's eighteen-year-old maid-of-honour, Catherine Howard, a cousin of Anne Boleyn. By this time, he had begun to act platonically towards his wife, treating her more like a sister than a lover. Anne of Cleves, for her part, was content to comfort herself with drink.

Catherine could not have been more different from Anne. She was not modest and pious, but fresh and passionate. Certainly, she was no innocent. Having lost her mother at an early age, she had been brought up by her step-grandmother, the Dowager Duchess of Norfolk, at Horsham in Sussex. The house was a large and crowded establishment, where numerous young relatives were packed together in dormitories. These were the scenes of frequent romantic assignations and midnight feasts that often ended in communal love-play. Catherine took her first lover when she was just fourteen. Her seducer was Henry Manox, a music teacher who, ironically enough, pounced on her during one of her virginal lessons. Catherine later claimed that full sex had not taken place, but 'at the flattering and fair persuasions of Manox, being by a young girl, I suffered him at sundry times to handle and touch the secret parts of my body which neither became me with honesty to permit nor him to require.' Manox, too, swore that he never knew her 'carnally', though he admitted that he had made advances to her in a small sacristy behind the altar in the Duchess's chapel.

When the family moved to Norfolk House in Lambeth, Catherine met a new love, Francis Dereham. Soon the couple were playfully calling each other 'wife' and 'husband'. The house, which was a warren of galleries and tiny chambers, was ideal for their amorous trysts.

Catherine's own descriptions of what went on is explicit enough: 'Francis Dereham by many persuasions procured me to his vicious purpose and obtained first to lie upon my bed with his doublet and hose and after within the bed and, finally, he lay with me naked and used me in such sort as a man doth his wife many and sundry times, but how often I know not.'

Dereham and his friend, Edward Waldegrave, found a way of secretly entering the maiden's chamber at night, staying there till dawn with their respective loves, Catherine and Joan Bulmer. Dereham and Catherine would, it was reported, 'kiss and hang by their bellies as if they were two sparrows.' Love tokens were exchanged and, in the dark, there was a great deal of 'puffing and blowing'. Despite her youth, Catherine was so experienced that she knew 'how a woman might meddle with a man and yet conceive no child unless she would herself.'

These erotic games went to some extremes. Another member of the household, Katherine Tylney, later admitted that on occasions she had joined Dereham and Catherine in bed, in an intimate *ménage à trois*.

Although Catherine's behaviour was widely known, it was quickly hushed up when she caught the King's eye. To Henry, the girl was a 'blushing rose without a thorn', a 'perfect Jewel of womanhood', and he lavished expensive gifts upon her. Catherine could easily have become yet another of the King's mistresses, but the powerful and ambitious Howard family saw Henry's infatuation as a way of ridding the country of its protestant queen and as a means of personal advancement.

By this stage, Cromwell had conceded that the marriage which he had so carefully arranged was no longer serving any purpose. 'You should never have any more children, for the comfort of the realm, if you should so continue,' he told the King.

Once this decision had been reached, the convocation of clerics swiftly announced the findings that the king required. They declared that 'there had been no carnal copulation between Your Majesty and the said Lady Anne, nor with that just impediment interceding could it be possible.' The King was not permanently impotent, they decided. Rather, his sexual problem was a result of his troubled conscience. Anne had previously been promised to someone else and this made the match morally and legally repugnant to him. The marriage was quickly annulled, although Anne was forced to remain in England. In all probability, she took other lovers. Rumour had it that she became pregnant twice and actually gave birth to an illegitimate child.

Once more, and official dispensation had to be arranged before Henry's wedding with Catherine could proceed, as he had had carnal knowledge of her first cousin, Anne Boleyn. When that had been obtained, the King now fifty, married his nineteen-year-old mistress. The ceremony was organised in some haste because, as the French ambassador wrote, Catherine was already '*enceinte*' – that is, big with child. But whose child was it? The King, though his desires might be youthful, was fat, sick and bald. He waist swelled out to a massive 54 inches, and Catherine had already shown a preference for younger, slimmer men.

The court was soon packed with Catherine's adolescent playmates, among them Joan Bulmer and Katherine Tylney, but unfortunately one of them had been overlooked – Mary Lassels. She had been one of the gentlewomen in the service of the Duchess of Norfolk and had shared Catherine's communal bedroom at Lambeth. Egged on by her brother, a protestant who sought to end the influence of the Catholic Howard family, Mary told the Archbishop of Canterbury, Thomas Cranmer, about Catherine's youthful indiscretions.

Under torture, both Manox and Dereham admitted their passionate encounters with Catherine and the latter also revealed that Thomas Culpepper, a gentleman of the King's Privy Chamber, had 'succeeded him in the Queen's affections'.

Culpepper was something of a royal favourite. According to the French ambassador, he had been brought up from childhood in the King's household and 'ordinarily shared his bed.' Apparently, he 'wished to share the Queen's bed too,' the Frenchman added mischievously.

This was not the first time that the young man had been in trouble. On a previous occasion, he had raped the wife of a park-keeper in a secluded thicket, while three or four of his servants held her down. Henry had pardoned him for that offence, but this time he would show no mercy.

Whilst stretched on the rack, Culpepper claimed that Catherine's attendant Lady Jane Rochford – who had given such eloquent testimony about Anne Boleyn's adultery with her husband – had 'provoked' him into the liaison. Despite the torture, though, he continued to deny that he had ever enjoyed full carnal knowledge of the Queen.

When questioned, Catherine also accused Lady Rochford, saying that she had encouraged her to flirt – though like Thomas, she also denied actual adultery. Lady Rochford, meanwhile, condemned them both as adulterous while, simultaneously, maintaining that she had no knowledge of the affair.

However, it was Katherine Tylney's evidence that tipped the scales. She revealed that the Queen had often stayed out of her chamber at night, running up the back stairs to Culpepper's room until two in the morning. Soon the dungeons in the Tower of London were so full that the royal apartments there had to be turned over to accommodate the new influx of prisoners.

Dereham and Culpepper were convicted of treason at the Guildhall and sentenced to be hanged, drawn and quartered. Both appealed for mercy to the King. As a result, Culpepper's sentence was commuted to beheading. His was the lesser crime in Henry's eyes. Dereham, however, had besmirched his virgin bride and was doomed to pay the full, barbaric forfeit. The heads of both victims were fixed on poles on London Bridge and could still be seen there, stripped of their flesh, as much as four years later.

Catherine was robbed of her royal title, on account of her 'carnal copulation' with Dereham. She was also indicted for having led 'an abominable, base, carnal, voluptuous and vicious life' and for acting 'like a common harlot with divers persons ... while maintaining the outward appearance of chastity and honesty'.

On 13th February 1542, Catherine Howard was beheaded at Tower Green, on the very same block where her cousin, Anne Boleyn, had met her end. She was followed on to the scaffold by the conniving Lady Rochford, while the block was still wet with her mistress's blood.

The King of France was greatly amused by the tales of Catherine's misconduct, declaring: 'She hath done wondrous naughty.' He took the opportunity to send Henry a sarcastic sermon condemning the 'lightness of women'.

Even after all these mishaps, Henry had still not tired of the opposite sex. After Catherine's execution he attended a 'great supper' with twenty-six ladies at his table and another thirty-five at a table near by. One, in particular, caught his eye – Anne Basset. A 'pretty young thing with wit enough to do as badly as the others if she were to try,' said the French ambassador.

However, by now, women were growing more than a little wary of Henry – his two divorces and two executions provided a quite considerable deterrent. 'In what a slippery estate there were, if the King after receiving them to bed, should, through any mistake, declare them no maids,' it was said at the time.

Henry soon reached desperation point. He even considered having Anne of Cleves back in his bed.

Scurrilous rumours to this effect circulated on the Continent, but the King's advisers soon realized that this was no solution. If, by some miracle, he had managed to father an heir with her, it would have caused grave constitutional problems with the succession.

Finally, instead of running the risk of picking another young bride, Henry turned to a woman whose virginity could not be in question. She had twice been widowed.

Catherine Parr was, like all his English brides a distant cousin – though this says rather more about the narrowness of aristocratic society than it does about any subconscious urge to commit incest on Henry's part. She had first been married at the tender age of seventeen – to a madman, Edward Broughton, who died in 1532. A childless widow, she then married Lord Latimer, who was a good twenty years her senior and only two years younger than the King.

For most of their ten years of marriage, Lord Latimer was an invalid. Then, when he was finally on his death bed, she fell passionately in love with Jane Seymour's dashing but unscrupulous brother, Thomas, and hoped to marry him after her husband died. By this stage, however, Henry was already showing an interest in her and he pursued her while Latimer was still alive.

Even though Catherine's affections lay elsewhere, there was no disobeying the King's command. So, on 12th July 1543, Henry VIII was married for the last time.

This new match ruffled a few feathers. Catherine was no beauty and while Anne of Cleves had felt neither humiliated nor surprised by Henry's decision to marry pretty young Catherine Howard, this latest union seemed like a blatant insult. After all, Henry could not be marrying Catherine in order to beget an heir.

The King was now so fat that three large men could fit into his doublet. Besides, Catherine Parr had already been through two marriages without producing any issue. Anne offered to waive her generous pension, provided that she could go home to Cleves. But, while the King lived, she was never allowed to leave England.

The King made no secret of the fact that he had had his fill of young wives and was marrying purely for companionship. So Queen Catherine took up residence in a small bedroom next to his – a sure sign that Henry regarded her as a nursemaid rather than a bedmate. Either way, she made the old King content until his death on 7th February 1547.

Henry had been injured in a jousting accident in 1524 and suffered from a badly ulcerated leg for the rest of his life. This caused him much pain, especially as he put on weight when he grew older. It is probable that love-making was a painful experience for him.

Despite this, and his intermittent impotence, the King continued throughout his reign to try to sire more sons – using younger women in the hope that they would be more fertile. Henry knew all too well that the country had been torn apart in the past by questions of succession and that these problems would be multiplied if the heir to the throne was a woman.

2

THE AGE OF
INNOCENTS

Born in 1537, the sickly child of Jane Seymour, Prince Edward was always a pawn in the game of politics. When he was just six, plans were already being drawn up for his marriage to Mary Queen of Scots, in the Treaty of Greenwich.

This was not the first Anglo-Scottish match to have been proposed. Nineteen years earlier, Edward's sister, Mary, had been promised to James V of Scotland. But the English had hung back, fearing that their northern neighbour would attempt to take control of the whole country.

In 1543, the Scottish people took against the Treaty of Greenwich for the same reason. They did not want to see their nation swallowed up by the English Crown. Henry's next attempt to marry off his son occurred in 1546, after war with France had been concluded. The King hoped to secure the peace by matching his son with a powerful ally. The Duke of Holstein offered one

31

of his daughters and there were negotiations concerning a Habsburg princess, but both these options were dismissed when Charles V offered one of his many nieces. These dealings were halted by the King's death.

Meanwhile, on 25th June 1547, Henry's widow Catherine married her beloved Seymour – even though the latter had proposed to both the young Princesses, Mary and Elizabeth, and had been rejected by their father. An ambitious man, Seymour had also once boasted of his intention of marrying Anne of Cleves. He was reputed to be 'one of the prettiest men in court' and these good looks caused his name to be linked with a number of eligible women, among them Mary, Duchess of Richmond. Seymour had wisely stayed out of the country while Henry was alive, but within five months of the King's death he had returned to resume his secret meetings with Catherine.

'When it shall be your pleasure to repair hither, you must take some pains to come early in the morning, that you may be gone again by seven o'clock,' she wrote to her lover. 'And so, I suppose you may come without suspicion. I pray you let me know overnight at what hour you come, that your porteress may wait at the gate to the fields for you.'

Catherine's love-match soon bore fruit. At the age of 35, after three childless marriages, she conceived. Typically enough, while she was pregnant, her errant husband sought diversion elsewhere. He found this in the arms of his fifteen-year-old stepdaughter, Elizabeth. Seymour would enter her room while she was dressing, pat her on the behind and then steal the key of her chamber, so that she could not escape. He would then tickle her until she screamed for mercy and would romp with her in the gardens, even under the gaze of his pregnant wife.

Some mornings, he would enter her room, dressed only in a short nightshirt, and fling back the curtains of her four-poster bed. On one occasion he tore her gown into shreds while Catherine herself held Elizabeth down. After that the child was sent away. It was rumoured that Catherine had surprised the pair in a passionate embrace.

Somerset, the Lord Protector, Seymour's elder brother, saw all too clearly what he had in mind – to marry Princess Elizabeth when Catherine was dead and take the throne beside her.

As the time of her delivery drew near, Catherine left for her country estate at Hansworth, accompanied by Lady Jane Grey and several other maid-servants. 'Mary Odell being abed with me laid her hand upon my belly to feel it stir,' she wrote to Seymour. 'It hath stirred these three days every morning and evening so that I trust when you come it will make you some pastime.'

On 30th August 1548, Catherine gave birth to a daughter. The child was healthy but the Queen Dowager herself felt ill. In her fever, she made paranoid ravings about her husband and the gentlewomen around her. Even when Seymour lay down beside her to comfort her, she continued with her accusations. She died six days later.

The faithless Seymour did not survive his wife by long. In 1549, he was executed for sedition, after trying to murder Edward VI in his chamber. Princess Elizabeth was also implicated in this plot, because of her intimate relations with Seymour.

When Edward VI acceded to the throne in 1547, he was still unmarried – at the grand old age of ten. The young prince was, by all accounts, rather good looking. One foreign envoy described him as 'an angel in human form ... it is almost impossible to imagine a more beautiful face and figure.' He had a very fair complexion, grey eyes and, as a youth, the beginnings of a light auburn beard. His clear skin was his chief claim to beauty and his courtiers tried to emulate it by artificial means, dyeing and plucking their eyebrows. Some would be bled two or three times a year in an attempt to achieve the right pallid effect. Edward was also thought to be very priggish. He once wrote to his half-sister Mary, instructing her to 'attend no longer foreign dances and merriments, which do not become a Christian princess.'

In 1552, Edward was formally betrothed to Princess Elizabeth of France. His advisers were keen for him to marry, but counselled him against using marriage as a tool for cementing alliances – as that 'causes much whoredom and divorcing,' warned the Bishop of Worcester. With the memory of his father's marital discord clearly in mind, Edward was urged to 'not choose a proud wanton' but 'to find it in your heart to love and lead your life in pure and chaste espousage' with Elizabeth.

Although the engagement was a diplomatic rather than a romantic affair, Edward did seem to have love uppermost in his thoughts at the time. That Christmas, he attended the revels at Greenwich, of which the highlight was a pageant called the Triumph of Cupid.

The arrangement with the French Princess did not prevent Edward from going against his advisers' wishes, by exploring the possibilities of the Scottish match that his father had wanted so much. Accordingly, he invited the 35-year-old Mary of Guise, The Regent of Scotland, to visit him at the Palace of Westminster. When she knelt before him in the Great Hall, he raised her up and kissed her on both cheeks. He also kissed all the ladies in her party.

Edward also organised a grand banquet in her honour, arranged concerts and showed her around the royal gardens and galleries. All the time, he pressed her on the question of marriage to her daughter Mary Stuart, who was, in fact, already engaged to the Dauphin of France. 'Such a fashion of dealing is not the nearest way to a woman's heart,' she warned the youth. 'Your Majesty should have approached me more gently.'

After this rebuff, Edward fell back on his plans to marry the Princess Elizabeth. He sent her a diamond ring and a portrait of himself, which she was instructed to hang in her bedroom. But all these plans came to nothing. In 1553 he died before he could taste the pleasures of the marriage bed.

His successor, Lady Jane Grey, was almost as innocent as Edward and certainly showed no eagerness to consummate her own marriage – only doing so when ordered to by the Duke of Northumberland. At the time of her birth, in October 1537, she was fifth in line for the throne and her parents nurtured ambitions for her to marry Prince Edward. She was brought up in Thomas Seymour's household and seems to have had a crush on the older man. However, as she blossomed into a young woman, she had no shortage of suitors, all of them keen to improve their social status. Seymour kept them at bay, arguing that 'Lady Jane should not be married until such time as she should be able to bear a child, and her husband to get one.' To protect her further, he also spread the rumour that he was going to marry her himself.

Seymour seems to have had the same boisterous relationship with her that he had enjoyed with Elizabeth – to whom he wrote, enquiring 'if her great buttocks had grown any less or no'. Given his reputation for debauchery, there were doubts about leaving Jane in Seymour's care. However, when she eventually departed from his household, she wrote to thank him for his 'great goodness' and for having been like a 'loving and kind father to her'.

By then, the young heiress was a considerable beauty. She had been the belle of the ball when she attended Edward VI's reception for Mary of Guise. She had a fine shapely figure, delicate features, a sensuous mouth and inviting red lips. Her arched eyebrows and cascading hair were a striking auburn colour, and her freckles stood out well against her pale skin. However, it was her lively manner and her youthful enthusiasm that made the greatest impact on her contemporaries.

Inevitably, her beauty and innocence attracted predators. The scheming Duke of Northumberland was much taken with her, and decided to marry her off to his fifth son, Lord Guildford Dudley, a witless but ambitious adolescent.

Northumberland had effectively controlled the government for the previous two years. He realized that the King was sick and that his days were numbered. So he decided to enhance his family's fortunes by pushing through the betrothal of his son to Lady Jane. When she was told of this, the girl refused point blank to marry him. Such disobedience was unheard of in the sixteenth century. Jane argued that she was already contracted to marry Lord Hertford, but her parents bullied her, and eventually the 'blows from her mother and curses from her father' succeeded in forcing her into the match. Her sister married Lord Hertford secretly nine years later.

Jane's marriage was just one element in a complex system of dynastic alliances arranged by Northumberland. At the same time, he married off Jane's thirteen-year-old sister Katherine to Lord Herbert and Katherine Dudley to Lord Hastings. Jane's youngest sister, eight-year-old Mary, was also betrothed to her cousin, Arthur Grey, and the couple were to be married as soon as she reached puberty.

Jane's wedding was a splendid affair. The bride wore a gown of silver and gold brocade encrusted with diamonds and gleaming pearls were plaited into her shoulder-length hair. There were jousts, masques and feasts but, after all these lavish festivities, the groom succumbed to food poisoning and the marriage was not consummated.

Time went by and soon Edward was on his deathbed. Northumberland acted quickly. He persuaded the dying King to alter the succession in favour of Lady Jane Grey and ordered that the marriage be consummated immediately. Within weeks, the couple were publicly 'abedded'. Not surprisingly, Jane did not take kindly to this. Soon afterwards she withdrew to the Palace at Chelsea to take a 'recreation' or cure.

When Edward died, Lady Jane Grey was proclaimed Queen. Her reign lasted just nine days, before Mary, Henry's daughter by Catherine of Aragon, swept to power. Jane and Guildford were arrested and confined to the Tower. They were tried. He was sentenced to be hanged, drawn and quartered; she to being burned.

Mary felt merciful and would have let them live if Sir Thomas Wyatt had not organized a protestant rebellion against her proposed marriage to the Catholic Philip of Spain. Even so, their sentences were commuted to beheading. In the Tower, Jane refused to meet with her handsome young husband, but she watched his decapitated torso being hauled back from Tower Hill. She then had to submit to the degrading ordeal of an 'examination by a body of matrons' to check if she was pregnant, before losing her head from a single stroke of the axe on Tower Green.

3

THE KINKY
QUEENS

Given all the sexual activities of their father, it would hardly have been surprising if Henry VIII's two surviving daughters had developed warped attitudes towards affairs of the heart. During the uncertain days before she came to the throne, Mary chose to surround herself with women, among them Mary Brown 'whom for her virtue I love'.

During the reign of Edward VI, Mary expanded her entourage. 'The Household of the Princess was the only harbour for honourable young gentlewomen given any way to piety and devotion,' reported Jane Dormer, one of her handmaidens, 'and the greatest Lords in the Kingdom were suitors to her to receive their daughters in her service.'

Jane slept in Mary's chamber, wore some of Mary's jewels and carved meat for her mistress. In fact, the pair were so devoted that Mary dreaded the thought of Jane marrying and leaving her side. She would often say that

Jane Dormer deserved a good husband, but that she did not know any man good enough for her. When she was Queen, Mary even prevented Jane's marriage to Henry Courtenay, the most eligible bachelor in the kingdom. Only near the end of her reign did Mary allow her favourite lady-in-waiting to marry the Spanish envoy, the Duke of Feria.

Henry Courtenay seemed such a fine catch that many thought he would be a suitable match for Mary. But when she came to the throne at the age of 37 Mary dismissed the Handsome Courtenay as an effete youth. Instead, her ladies-in-waiting talked of little else but her forthcoming marriage to Philip of Spain. Courtenay sought to prevent this foreign match and was banished after his suspected involvement in Wyatt's rebellion, which aimed to end any alliance with Catholic Spain. The rebellion was put down with the usual grisly consequences and Courtenay died in exile.

Philip arrived at Southampton on 18th July 1554. He took one disparaging look at his bride, who was ten years his senior, and asked to see the rest of her household. He surveyed the flower of English womanhood with a critical eye and kissed each of them in turn.

Generally, his verdict was unfavourable. 'Those I have seen in the Palace have not struck me as being handsome,' declared one of Philip's courtiers, echoing his master's view. 'Indeed, they are downright ugly.'

'They are not women for whom the Spaniards need put themselves out of the way in entertaining or spending money on them, which is a very good thing for the Spaniards,' wrote another.

However, Philip's retainers were more impressed by the short skirts that the Englishwomen wore – 'they really look quite indelicate when they are seated.' With their Latin background, they were equally shocked by the way that the British thought nothing of showing their legs, kissing strangers on first acquaintance and, even, dining alone with their husband's male friends. Most brazen of all, in Spanish eyes, was the excellence that Englishwomen displayed at horse-riding.

Philip himself had a reputation for being tactful in dealing with unattractive women, but his attempts to flirt with Magdalen Dacre, one of Mary's maids of honour, were firmly rejected.

This was a foretaste of the problems that were to come. In the months that followed Mary's wedding ceremony, the Queen's advisers anxiously awaited the news that a royal heir was on the way. At last, in September 1554, it was announced that Mary was pregnant. At Easter 1555, a flock of Spanish ladies had gathered at Hampton Court to witness the birth. By the end of May, however, it was rumoured that Mary was not pregnant at all. The official line was that the original date of conception had been miscalculated. The fiction was still being maintained in July, by which time Hampton Court stank from its prolonged occupation. (In those days, the sanitation was very primitive, so normally the court was kept constantly on the move, to allow the royal palaces to be cleaned and fumigated.)

Eventually, in August, the Queen had to admit that she was deluding herself and that it was a phantom pregnancy. When this was announced Philip set sail back to Spain. Mary say him off at Greenwich. She put a brave face on his departure in public, but back in her apartments she broke down and wept.

She wrote letters imploring him to return. He did so, in March 1557, but as an ally rather than a loving husband. Philip wanted Mary to back him in his war against France. She did and, as a result, England loss possession of Calais.

When Philip left in January 1558, Mary once again thought she was pregnant. In fact, she was experiencing symptoms of dropsy, the disease that was about to kill her.

Mary was succeeded by Elizabeth I, the Virgin Queen, who was, in all probability, not a virgin at all. When she was just sixteen, there were rumours that she was pregnant by Thomas Seymour, Catherine Parr's ambitious husband.

Once she came to power, Elizabeth was beset with the customary royal problem of producing an heir to secure the succession. There was no shortage of potential husbands. Numerous foreign princes proposed to her, anxious to forge a political alliance. Even her widowed brother-in-law, Philip II of Spain, made an approach. One of the strongest contenders was Austria's Archduke Charles, who went to the extent of commissioning François Borth, a young man 'on very friendly terms with all the ladies of the bedchamber', to report back any mention that the Queen might make of him.

When she first acceded, Elizabeth showed little interest in men. Perhaps her affair with Seymour or her father's philandering had put her off. Instead, she surrounded herself with unmarried women who would dance for their mistress and who slept in her private chamber. Elizabeth went through fits of jealousy if any of these ladies elected to leave her service in order to marry. Katherine Grey was sent to the Tower for this and

Thomas Perrot's marriage to Lady Dorothy Devereux earned him nine months in Marshalsea prison.

Then, about a year after she came to the throne, she embarked on a relationship with Lord Robert Dudley. The pair had been born on the same day in September 1533 and had known each other intimately since childhood. They had even been imprisoned together in the Tower of London for part of Mary's reign.

Dudley's influence on the Queen was no secret. 'During the last few days, Lord Robert has come so much into favour that he does what he likes with affairs,' the Spanish ambassador reported in April 1559. 'It is even said that Her Majesty visits him in his chamber day and night.' The only problem with this was that Dudley was already married. His wife, Amy Robsart, had been picked for him by his family. His status matched her dowry. It was not in any sense a love match, and the retiring Amy lived in the country, where she was rarely visited by her husband.

There were rumours, however, that Dudley's marriage was not a long term problem. 'People go so far as to say that his wife has a malady of the breasts and the Queen is only waiting for her to die to marry Lord Robert,' was the comment of the Spanish ambassador. 'Sometimes Elizabeth speaks like a woman who will only accept a great prince ... then they say she is in love with Lord Robert and will never let him leave her.'

But then calamity struck. Amy was found dead at the foot of the stairs in her Berkshire home. Dudley was immediately suspected of murdering her. There was talk that the Queen herself was implicated and that Elizabeth had no alternative but to cool her ardour. From then on, she decided to keep Dudley at arm's length.

This produced limited results. Four years later, when the Queen rewarded Dudley with the earldom of Leicester, she had to complain to the Spanish ambassador that she was being treated insultingly: 'I am spoke of as if I am an immodest woman. I ought not to wonder at it. I have favoured him because of his excellent disposition and his many merits, but I am young and he is young, and therefore we have both been slandered. God knows they do us grievous wrong.'

The scandal over Amy's death effectively ruled out Dudley as a husband, allowing other ambitious suitors to press their claims. Sir William Pickering seemed a likely candidate for some time. He had charm, good looks and a reputation as a womanizer.

Pickering, however, was soon supplanted by Sir Christopher Hatton, a handsome young lawyer from Northampton. He wrote to the Queen with great passion: 'My spirit and soul, I feel, agreeth with my body and life, that to serve you is heaven; but to lack you is more than hell's torment unto them ... Would God I were with you but for one hour! ... Bear with me, my dear sweet lady; passion overcometh me ... Love me, for I love you ... Your bondsman, everlastingly tied.'

Nevertheless, Hatton was, in turn, swiftly replaced, first by Thomas Heneage, a gentleman of the Queen's Privy chamber, then by Edward Vere, Earl of Oxford, who showered her with gifts from his travels. The latter seemed a likely marriage prospect for a time, until he started pursuing several of the Queen's maids-of-honour and becoming involved in public brawls.

Sir Walter Raleigh's name was also linked with the Queen's, until he seduced a lady of the bedchamber, Elizabeth Throckmorton. The diarist John Aubrey wrote of their first sexual encounter describing how Sir Walter 'loved a wench well and, one time, getting up one of the maids of honour against a tree in a wood ('twas his first lady) who seemed at first boarding to be fearful of her honour, and modest, she cried, "Sweet Sir Walter, what do you me ask? Will you undo me? Nay sweet Sir Walter!" At last, as the danger and pleasure at the same time grew higher, she cried in the ecstasy "Swisser Swatter! Swisser Swatter!" She proved with child.'

Meanwhile, Elizabeth's attention was focused once more on Dudley and there were signs that she planned to marry him off to the recently widowed Mary Queen of Scots. Certainly the Queen was becoming more possessive about him. She was particularly upset when Dudley began toying with other ladies of the court. His enemies spread the rumour that he would pay as much as £300 to 'seek pasture among the waiting gentlewomen of her Majesty's great chamber'. In 1570, Dudley broke off his affair with Lady Frances Howard in order to woo Lady Douglas Sheffield, a cousin of the Queen and 'a lady of great beauty'.

'Being much taken with her perfections,' he soon enjoyed 'the unlawful fruition of her bed and body.' She became his mistress. Shortly afterwards, her husband died – poisoned, it was said, by Dudley.

The gossip increased when, in 1574, Lady Sheffield presented him with a son.

In retaliation, Elizabeth began entertaining overtures from the French King's younger brother Henry, Duke of Anjou, who was half her age, a staunch Catholic and a notorious bisexual. When that fell through – because of his refusal to renounce his faith – Elizabeth's affections turned to Henry's younger brother, the Duke of Alençon, who was prepared to show rather more flexibility on this question.

By this time, Dudley had become estranged from Lady Sheffield and the Queen seems to have entertained new hope there – only for it to be dashed by Jean Simier, an envoy of the Duke of Alençon. He revealed that Dudley had now taken up with Lettice, Countess of Essex, another of the Queen's cousins. According to the Spanish ambassador, she was a passionate red-head and 'one of the best looking ladies of the court'.

Elizabeth scolded Lettice for her disloyalty and sent Dudley off on a military campaign against the Irish. When he returned, however, the affair with Lettice continued. Rumour had it that he was the real father of her children. Then, when Lettice's husband died suddenly from dysentery, there was talk, once again, that Dudley had poisoned his rival. Lettice and Dudley were secretly married in 1578, weeks before the birth of their first legitimate child.

When the Queen heard about the wedding, she did her best to break the marriage. Even though Lady Sheffield had long been out of favour because of her affair with Dudley, she was now hauled before the Royal Councillors following accusations that she was his wife, as she had once claimed. However, since that liaison, Lady Sheffield had married Sir Edward Stafford and had no wish to jeopardize that match.

Elizabeth tried to mask her disappointment. When the Duke of Alençon visited England in 1579, she appeared to be captivated by him. During his stay, Elizabeth invited Dudley back to court so that he could witness her wooing her new lover. The Duke fell ill and the Queen nursed him back to health with her own hand, and even called him her pet 'frog'. But the puritan preacher John Stubbs railed against the possibility of their union, comparing the Duke of Alençon to the serpent 'coming to seduce the English Eve and ruin the English paradise'. Now nearing the menopause, Elizabeth may have had her own doubts about the relationship, fearing the rigours of childbirth.

In 1581, the Duke visited England again. This time Elizabeth announced that she would marry him, but her ladies-in-waiting 'lamented and bewailed and did so terrify and vex her mind that she spent the night in doubts and cares without sleep.' In the morning, she told her young suitor that the marriage was off.

Robert Dudley eventually died in 1588. Only then was Elizabeth reconciled with her cousin Lettice. 'My Lady Leicester was at court,' Rowland White reported to Sir Robert Sidney, 'she kissed the Queen's hand, and her breast, and she did embrace her.'

Lettice was accompanied by her son Robert Devereux, the Earl of Essex. He was a handsome, charming young man and, like his stepfather before him, he began to woo the Queen. Although flattered, the Queen knew that there was nothing behind the sweet words. Her teeth were decaying, her face wrinkled and a bright auburn wig hid her thinning hair. The young man was under no illusions about this. On returning from an expedition, Essex once shoved past her guards and barged into her chamber when she was only just out of bed; still undressed, hairless and without her make-up.

The court at that time was full of other, more comely diversions. Lady-in-waiting Anne Vavasour was earning a formidable reputation for promiscuity, eventually being sent to the Tower after giving birth to the illegitimate son of the Earl of Oxford. Later she married, but left her husband to become the mistress of Sir Henry Lee, presenting him, too, with a bastard son. After his death, she married again, only to be charged with bigamy and fined £200.

The father of Mary Fitton, another lady-in-waiting, asked Sir William Knollys to protect her virtue. He duly promised to 'defend the innocent lamb from the wolfish cruelty and fox-like subtlety of the tame beasts of this place.' But Sir William turned out to be an old wolf himself and seduced the maid. However, he was already married and informed Mary that he could not be with her until 'the old tree be cut down'. Mary was not at all impressed, replying that 'while the grass is growing the horse may starve.' She promptly began an affair with William Herbert, the son of Lord Pembroke.

In order to meet her lover, Mary would steal away from the court by dressing up as a man. However, in February 1601, her swelling belly gave her away. Herbert, by then the Earl of Pembroke, admitted that he was the father of the child but 'utterly renounceth all marriage' and was sent to the Fleet prison. There, he wrote a verse blaming Mary for his downfall:

> Then this advice, fair creature, take from me
> Let none pluck fruit unless he plucks the tree
> For if with one, with thousands thou'lt turn whore
> Break ice in one place and it cracks the more.

Mary was taken back in disgrace to the country by her father, who declared: 'Such shame as never had Cheshire woman.'

In this debauched atmosphere, Essex's romantic approaches to the Queen seemed out of place. Instead, in 1590, he secretly married Sir Philip Sidney's widow. When she heard about this, Elizabeth soon forgave him and allowed Lady Essex to be present at court. However, her generosity made her all the more vexed when Essex ignored both her and his wife and started chasing several of her ladies-in-waiting.

First he seduced Elizabeth Southwell and made her pregnant. Then he flirted so openly with Elizabeth Brydges, daughter of Lord Chandos, that the Queen had to expel her from the court.

Next, he embarked on an affair with Lady Mary Howard, who flaunted herself before him so brazenly that it was clear she wished 'more to win the Earl than her mistress's goodwill'. The Queen was so outraged that she borrowed one of Lady Mary's dresses and wore it herself. As the girl was considerably slimmer than the ageing Queen, this failed to impress the young man. Elizabeth was so incensed that she confiscated the dress, swearing that she would no longer tolerate 'such ungracious flouting wenches'.

The Queen eventually forgave Essex his adulterous escapades, but she could not afford to be so generous when, in 1599, he was accused of spreading sedition in Ireland. However, she stopped short of sending him to trial for treason and instead had him severely censured at a private court of justice. Unrepentant, Essex and a small band of followers rode into London, planning to capture the Tower, raise support in the City, then seize the Queen. But the Palace of Westminster had been barricaded and support for the rebel quickly dwindled. Essex made a last stand at his London mansion, but was forced to surrender. He was convicted of high treason and sentenced to death.

Even then, it was said, the Queen might have saved him. She had once given him a ring which, she had promised, would absolve him from any crime. He sent it to her, but on its way, it fell into the hands of one of his enemies, Lady Nottingham. She held on to it until it was too late, only passing it to the Queen after Essex had been beheaded.

On her deathbed, in March 1603, Elizabeth named her cousin James VI of Scotland as her heir. Beside her as she died was a small casket, containing the last letter she had received from Robert Dudley.

In 1559, the Queen had asked Sir John Mason to instruct the House of Commons to erect 'a marble stone which shall declare that a Queen lived and died a virgin'. Although Elizabeth I was known as the Virgin Queen, no such monument was ever put in place.

There were sound political reasons why Elizabeth never took a husband, but her detractors preferred to spread more colourful rumours. It was alleged that her genitals were deformed or even that she was a hermaphrodite. During her lifetime, she herself complained of being 'of barren stock'. To have known that, she must have slept with at least one of her many suitors.

While Elizabeth's love life was a model of discretion, the same could not be said for Mary Queen of Scots. She was engaged to the Dauphin at the age of six and sent to France, where she was brought up in the debauched court so beloved of Mary Boleyn. There she was tutored by Queen Catherine de Medici, who main instrument of policy seems to have been the corruption of her own children. Mary married at fifteen. Three years later, when her husband died, she returned to Scotland. She was followed soon after by the poet Pierre de Chatelard, whom she was said to have 'loved completely'.

John Knox wrote in outrage that 'she would lie upon Chatelard's shoulder, and sometimes privily she would steal a kiss of his neck.' The poet had the misfortune to be discovered in Mary's bedroom on two occasions and was subsequently executed for his presumption.

When Elizabeth I tried to make a match between Mary and her own lover Robert Dudley, she found that Mary had already fallen for Henry Stuart, Lord Darnley. Sir James Melville described the latter as 'more like a woman than a man, for he was lovely, beardless and lady-faced'. The two were married in secret.

Mary soon realized that the wedding had been a terrible mistake. Although Darnley was, in her eyes, 'the properest and best proportioned long man' she had ever seen, he was in fact an alcoholic adulterer, who was suffering from syphilis.

Mary does not seem to have been fooled for long. Just four months after her marriage to Darnley, she was up 'playing cards until the small hours' with the musician David Rizzio. This proved to be a fatal mistake.

One evening, while Mary was having supper at Holyrood House with some friends, Darnley and a group of armed men burst in. They grabbed Rizzio, who tried clinging to Mary's skirts for protection. Despite this, he was dragged outside and stabbed to death on the stairway.

The murder created mayhem in Edinburgh and Mary decided to flee with Darnley. Six months later, she gave birth to a son, the future James VI of Scotland and James I of England.

However, the tension that had existed between Mary and Darnley was far from spent. Soon he was plotting to kidnap the child and seize the throne. One night, in Mary's absence, there was a terrific explosion and Darnley's near-naked body was found in a garden. His corpse had not been mutilated by the explosion, though, and it was clear that he had been strangled. Suspicion fell upon Lord Bothwell.

Bothwell was brought to trial, but found not guilty – perhaps because there was a large contingent of his soldiers stationed in Edinburgh at the time of the proceedings.

Less than three months after Darnley's murder, Mary was travelling from Stirling Castle to Edinburgh when she was abducted and raped by Bothwell. However, after he had divorced his first wife, Mary married him and they remained faithful to each other until they were parted in 1567. Bothwell went into exile and died in a Danish prison in 1578.

Mary was deposed in favour of her one-year-old son, James. She fled to England, where she was imprisoned by her cousin Elizabeth and her marriage was annulled in 1570.

In 1586, she was implicated in a plot against Elizabeth I, was tried and beheaded at Fotheringhay Castle in the following year. Her son made a few ineffective protests but, when he acceded to the English throne in 1603, he built a magnificent monument to her which still stands in Westminster Abbey today.

4

KINGS AND QUEENS

James I was not the first homosexual to gain the throne of England. William Rufus, the son of William the conqueror, had never made any secret of his preferences.

'Then was there flowing hair and extravagant dress,' wrote one dismayed cleric, 'and was invented the fashion of shoes with curved points; then the model for young men was to rival women in delicacy of person, to mind their gait, to walk with loose gesture, and half naked. Enervated and effeminate, they unwillingly remained what nature had made them, the assailers of others' chastity, prodigal of their own. Troops of pathetics and droves of whores followed in the Court.'

There was little mourning when William II died in a mysterious hunting accident.

Richard the Lionheart was cast in the same mould. He was urged by the clergy to leave off his unnatural vices and to live with his Spanish wife, but Richard I preferred to spend his time with the Crusaders in the Middle East, where homosexual practices were tolerated. His marriage was never consummated and his long-suffering queen eventually left him.

While Richard was busily engaged on his foreign expeditions his brother John made free with the wives and daughters of his barons. During his own reign, they eventually curtailed these outrages by forcing him to sign the Magna Carta. Predictably, King John took a less charitable view of his own wife's sexual indulgence. When Isabella of Angoulème took a lover, John had him and his two accomplices killed and their bodies draped over her bed as a warning.

Edward II was probably the most notorious of England's homosexual monarchs. Before coming to the throne, his first companion, Piers Gaveston, was banished by the Prince's father after Edward had tried to secure lands and a title for him. But after the King's death, Gaveston returned to become Keeper of the Realm and the Earl of Cornwall. Edward arranged Gaveston's marriage to his niece, while he himself wed the twelve-year-old Isabella of France. At the ceremonial feast, Edward and Gaveston caressed each other so openly that Isabella's uncles left in disgust.

Edward went to the extent of banning all other women from his court. He decreed that 'none of the King's meignee [household] of what condition so ever he be ... keep a wife at court, nor elsewhere as a follower to the court; but only such women to be there which are in chief with the king.'

Within nine months of Edward's succession to the throne, his barons were demanding Gaveston's exile.

Edward was too weak to resist these demands and accompanied Gaveston to his ship, kissing and fondling him until the moment of his departure.

Two years later though, Edward's political fortunes had improved and Gaveston returned, only to face a more concerted attempt to have him banished permanently. He left again, but within weeks it was rumoured that he was back and hiding in the royal apartments.

When Gaveston appeared openly at the King's side at the Christmas celebrations of 1311, the barons rebelled. Edward and Gaveston fled to Scotland, where Edward pleaded with Robert the Bruce to give his lover sanctuary. Robert refused. Gaveston was captured and beheaded.

Edward was said to have been overcome with grief, but he soon found consolation – with his own wife. Five months after Gaveston's execution, Queen Isabella gave birth to a son, the future Edward III.

For nine years, the King and Queen lived happily together, producing three more children. But then Edward fell in love with Hugh Despencer, whose father was another court favourite. Their attachment had disastrous consequences for his marriage. A rebellion was raised, but it was swiftly ended. The ringleader was executed and Queen Isabella fled to France. There she gathered English dissidents around her, taking Lord Roger Mortimer as her lover.

In spite of the rumours that he was trying to divorce her, Edward demanded Isabella's return to England. She replied: 'I feel that marriage is a joining together of man and woman, maintaining the undivided habit of life, and that someone has come between my husband and myself trying to break this bond; I protest that I will not return until this intruder is removed, but, discarding my marriage garment, shall assume the robes of widowhood and mourning until I am revenged.'

Isabella donned widow's weeds, while Mortimer mounted a masterly military campaign. Soon, Edward and the Despencers were trapped in Bristol. The elder Despencer was captured and executed, while Edward and Hugh tried to flee for Ireland. But the wind blew their boat back on to the Welsh coast, where they were captured. Hugh Despencer was tried and executed, while Edward was forced to abdicate in favour of his son. Later he was found dead in his cell. There was no evidence of poison or any sign of a stab wound on his body. The rumour soon circulated that if the corpse were to be intimately examined, burn marks would be found internally, in 'those parts in which he had been wont to take his vicious pleasure'. A red-hot poker had been forced into his rectum.

The heterosexual Edward III, who had three children by his mistress, Alice Perrers, as well as four by his wife, retained some affection for his father. When he came to the throne at sixteen, he had Mortimer arrested and put to death as a traitor.

Although William Rufus, Edward II and James I would now be thought of as homosexual or, at the very least, as bisexual, these terms did not come into the English language until the turn of the century. Before 1900, no one would have defined themselves by their sexual orientation or proclivities. During the Middle Ages, when courtly love was in vogue, knights and courtiers were expected to fall in love with unattainable maids while keeping themselves to the company of men. The attitude of the church was equally ironic, for although it condemned the love between two men, homosexuality was rife among the clergy.

Sodomy was against the law. James I himself condemned it as one of the sins that cannot be forgiven. In 1570, in Edinburgh, two men accused of sodomy were burned at the stake. However, in England at least, there seems to have been tacit acceptance of homosexual practices. In the 45 years of Elizabeth I's reign and the 23 years of James's rule, only six men in the Home Counties were indicted of sodomy – and only one convicted – even though a contemporary diarist recorded in London in 1622 that 'the sinne of sodomye' was frequent 'in this wicked cittye'.

The Scottish, by contrast, had more of a reputation as heterosexual fornicators. Mistresses and bastard sons abound in their history. When young James VI became King of Scotland, his regent was James Stuart, Earl of Moray, one of the many illegitimate sons of James V.

James VI of Scotland, who became James I of England, was brought up in exclusively male company. Nubile young girls were excluded from his presence by the strictures of the Presbyterian church. So James turned his attention to his male courtiers, frequently to be rebuffed. The Earl of Holland reportedly spurned the youthful King's advances 'by turning aside and spitting after the king had sladdered in his mouth'.

When James was just thirteen, a distant cousin, thirty-year-old Esmé Stuart, arrived from the court of the flagrantly homosexual King Henry III of France. On their first meeting, Esmé prostrated himself before the teenage monarch.

An eyewitness wrote: 'No sooner did the young King see him, but in that he was so neare allyed in bloud, of so renouned a Family, eminent ornaments of body and minde, took him up and embraced him in a most amorous manner, conferred on him presently a rich inheritance; and that he might be imployed in state-affairs, elected him one of his honourable Privy Counsell, Gentleman of his Bed-chamber and Governour of Dumbarton Castle.'

Esmé Stuart brought a much-needed dash of colour to the Scottish court. He brought with him French courtiers, who were known for their drunkenness and swearing. Soon, James created him Duke of Lennox, a sign of his rapidly growing influence. Moray had already been murdered and when the current regent, the Earl of Morton, was arrested and executed, Lennox became the King's most powerful adviser.

He had left behind him in France a Catholic wife and children and, as such, he was regarded as a threat by protestant England. An English diplomat expressed concern over James's 'younge yeres and strange affection to Lennox' while contemporaries noted that the King, 'having conceived an inward affection' for Lennox, 'entered in great familiarity and quiet purposes with him.'

The Scottish clergy was more blunt. They declared that 'the Duke of Lennox went about to draw the King into carnal lust.'

Scotland's protestant lords moved quickly. They kidnapped the King and forced Lennox into exile. Lennox wrote that he would rather die than go on living without James's love, while the King expressed his own grief in poetry, likening Lennox to a little bird, pursued by hunters:

Yet they followed fast
Till she betwix my leggs her selfe did cast,
For saving her from these, which her opprest,
Whose hote pursute, her suffred not to rest.

But for all his devotion, the young King did not
deprive himself of lovers, James Stewart, Earl of Arran,
was one favourite. Patrick, Master of Gray, who had
come from the French court with Esmé Stuart in 1579,
was another. In addition, Francis Stewart, Earl of
Bothwell, the nephew and heir of Mary Queen of Scots'
last husband, frequently embraced James in public and
the King was said to 'hang around his neck'. Another
one of James's circle of intimates was George Gordon,
the Earl of Huntley.

'The King went to the castle to dinner,' wrote an
English observer, 'where he entertained Huntley as well
and kindly as ever; yea, he kissed him at time to the
amazement of many.'

When the King fell out with Bothwell, accusing him of
witchcraft, Huntley sided with James – but then dis-
astrously later changed his mind and took Bothwell's
part. The two men eventually had to flee abroad.
Bothwell never returned, but Huntley submitted to the
King's will, returned to his affection and was rewarded
for this with the title of marquis.

With women James was 'but a cold wooer'. However,
for the sake of an heir, the twenty-three-year-old James
began a passionate correspondence with fifteen-year-
old Anne of Denmark. Soon he was 'far in love with the
Princess of Denmark, hearing of her beauty and virtues
and affection towards him'. Apparently, James gazed at
her picture nightly.

When Anne arranged to sail across to visit him in Scotland, only to be blown back by a storm, James appeared distraught, composing passionate love letters and sonnets – even though he had never met the supposed object of his affections. He also issued a proclamation declaring his intention to marry and explaining the delay. Despite these assurances, rumours circulated that James, like Elizabeth I, was 'of barren stock'.

Eventually, James decided to sail to Denmark and claim his bride. 'God is my witness I could not have abstained longer,' he wrote.

James and Anne married in Denmark in 1589. They returned to Scotland and the relationship remained stable until 1593, when Anne was pregnant. After the birth, they fell out over the upbringing of the heir, though they still went on to have two more sons and four more daughters.

James turned against his wife. Instead of writing love poetry, he turned his hand to 'A Satire against Women':

> *Even so all women are of nature vaine*
> *And can not keep no secrett unrevealed*
> *And where as once they doe concaive disdaine*
> *They are unable to be reconcealed*
> *Fullfild with talke and clatters but respect*
> *And often tymes of small or none effect.*

As the tensions within his marriage increased, James made very little attempt to conceal his true preferences. When he became King of England, he brought south with him a smooth-faced young man called James Hay as his master of the royal wardrobe.

Hay was very free with his master's new treasury and was soon replaced by Philip Herbert, an expert in the manly pursuit of hunting which James had always admired. When the King grew tired of him, Herbert, like Hay, was married off to a daughter of the English peerage. On the morning after the former's wedding, the King appeared in the couple's bedchamber in his nightshirt and clambered into bed with them.

With Herbert out of the way, other courtiers tried to entice James, in the hope of advancement. The most successful of these was a tall, good-looking page named Robert Carr. He came to the King's attention when he fell from his horse during a jousting tournament in full view of the King. James went to see whether he was injured and was immediately attracted to the youth.

Carr was put into the care of the King's physicians. James visited him daily and even tried to teach him Latin – though some wags suggested that his time would be better spent teaching the young Scot to speak English. Once Carr had recovered, they were inseparable. In 1607, Carr was knighted and became a gentleman of the bedchamber.

'The Prince leaneth on his arm, pinches his cheeks, smooths his ruffled garment, and when he looketh at Carr, directeth discourse to divers others,' wrote one witness.

Another said that James's relationship with Carr was not 'carried on with a discretion sufficient to cover lesse scandalous behaviour; for the king's kissing them after so lascivious a mode in publick, and upon the theatre, as it were, of the world, prompted many to imagine some things done in the trying-house, that exceed my expressions no lesse then they do my experience.'

Carr, of course, was eager for personal advancement. James complied by making him Lord of Rochester and by seeking to arrange an advantageous marriage with Frances, Lady Essex. Unfortunately she was already married, but her husband had been travelling abroad for four years on the Grand Tour. When he returned to claim her, Frances rebuffed his sexual advances with potions obtained from a magician and Carr pressed James to grant her a divorce.

In 1613, the King had the marriage annulled on the grounds of Lord Essex's alleged impotence, allowing Carr and Lady Essex to be united. At the wedding, she wore her hair loose over her shoulders to symbolize, disingenuously, her virginity and, at the wedding banquet, the lovers were serenaded with a singularly inappropriate song. One verse went as follows:

> Let us now sing of love's delight,
> For he alone is lord tonight;
> Some friendship between man and man prefer,
> But I th'affection between man and wife.
> What good can be in life,
> Whereof no fruites appeare?

And the chorus ran:

> That pleasure is of all bountiful and kind,
> That fades not straight, but leaves a living joy behinde.

After his marriage, Carr was created Earl of Somerset and used his influence to have Thomas Overbury, a former admirer of Lady Essex, imprisoned in the Tower. Overbury had the temerity to oppose Carr's ruthless ambition and was later found dead. He had been poisoned and the evidence pointed to Carr's involvement.

He and his wife were arrested. Tried and found guilty of murder, they were sentenced to death, although James commuted the sentence to imprisonment at his pleasure. They were released from the Tower seven years later, but Carr never saw the King again.

James's affections had long since turned to George Villiers, whom he nicknamed Steenie. This was a contraction of St Stephen who, according to the Bible, had a face that glowed like 'the face of an angel'.

According to Bishop Goodman, Villiers had a 'very lovely complexion; he was the handsomest bodied man in England'. This view was echoed by another courtier, who wrote: 'I saw everything in him full of delicacy and handsome features; yea his hands and face seemed to me especially effeminate and curious.' A third source, meanwhile, commented that James found in 'the disposition of his youth an unbounded levity and a ductile licentiousness'.

Villiers was the protégé of Philip Herbert, James's former lover, but he was not the only courtier who catered for the King's fancies. A rival faction used the Countess of Suffolk to procure 'choice young men who she daily curled and perfumed their breaths'.

This type of sexual politics was present at the highest levels. The Queen, who disliked Carr, helped Villiers to become a gentleman of the bedchamber and James was soon hopelessly in love with him.

In letters, he referred to Steenie as 'wife', 'husband', as well as 'child' and 'father'. He also told the Privy Council that he loved Villiers, whom he had just created Earl of Buckingham, more than any other man.

Buckingham responded in kind. In one of his letters he wrote: 'I shall never forgett at Franham where ye Bed's hed could not be found betwene your Master and his Doge.'

When Buckingham married, James wrote:

My only sweet and dear child,

Thy dear dad sends thee his blessing and also to his daughter. The Lord of Heaven sent you a sweet and blithe awakening, all kinds of comfort in your sanctified bed and bless the fruits thereof, that I may have sweet bedchamber boys to play with me (and this is my daily prayer).

Sweet hearty, when thou riseth, keep thee from importunity of people that may trouble thy mind, that meeting I may see thy white teeth shine upon me, and to bear me company in my journey; and so God bless thee. James R.

Naturally, Buckingham's arranged marriage did not end his affair with the King. In December 1624, towards the end of his life, James wrote to Buckingham: 'I pray God that I may have a joyful and comfortable meeting with you, and that we may make this Christmas a new marriage, ever to be kept hereafter; for, God so love me, as I desire only to live in this world for your sake, and that I had rather live banished in any part of the world with you than live a sorrowful widow's life without you. And so God bless you, my sweet child and wife, and grant that ye may ever be a comfort to your old dad and husband.'

The younger Buckingham may have grown tired of the physical demands of his aged and unattractive admirers. When James I died, it was rumoured that Villiers had poisoned him. Certainly, he had ample opportunity. During the King's last illness, it was Buckingham that nursed him. Had he so wished, it would have been a simple matter for him to tamper with the medicaments that had been prescribed for the already weakened King. By this stage, he also had a new patron and, perhaps, lover – James's own son, the future Charles I. The two men were certainly close.

As a teenager, Charles had been jealous of his father's favourite. Once he had sprayed Villiers with water from a fountain, ruining his new suit. The young prince was a late developer. As a child, he was troubled with 'the green sickness', a type of anaemia common in girls at puberty. When it was rumoured that he was having an adolescent fling with Anne Gawdy, the daughter of a Norfolk gentleman, the Spanish ambassador reported that this was most unlikely, as Charles had not 'yet had anything to do with love affairs'. He was also rumoured to be 'sterile'.

Contemporary accounts suggest that Charles was submissive, feminine and narcissistic, and that he frequently 'blushed like a modest maiden', eschewing hot sauces that might 'please the palate or raise the lust.' But by 1624, Charles had, like his father, begun to call Buckingham 'Steenie', addressing him in intimate letters as 'sweetheart'. The two were constant companions.

Francis Bacon declared that Buckingham was a 'noble instrument for the service, contentment, and the heart's ease both of father and son'. But he also had a warning for the royal favourite: 'You serve a gracious Master and a good', he said 'and there is a noble and hopeful Prince, whom you must not disserve; adore not him as the rising sun in such a measure, as that you put a jealousy into the father, who raised you.'

In fact, the growing affection between 'Steenie' and 'Baby Charles' did not make the King jealous, though he shed a tear when the two of them set off for Madrid to open marriage negotiations with the Infanta Maria, the daughter of the King of Spain. The success of this enterprise was threatened when Buckingham made a pass at the wife of their go-between, Count Olivares. The Countess agreed to an assignation with Buckingham, but sent in her place a 'notorious stew bird', that is, a prostitute.

Charles was favourably impressed with the Infanta and climbed over the palace wall at the Casa Del Campo in the hope of catching her without her chaperone. Unfortunately, the Infanta responded to this romantic approach by screaming loudly and running away.

She soon made it plain to her father that she would rather enter a nunnery than Charles's bed. Further obstacles were put in the way of the marriage and, eventually, Charles and Buckingham had to be rescued by the Royal Navy. When they were safely back in Britain, 'Steenie', 'Baby Charles' and his father treated the entire fiasco as a huge joke. For four hours after their reunion, peels of laughter could be heard echoing from inside the King's private chamber.

The heir to the throne still needed a wife, so Henry Rich, Baron Kensington, was sent to woo Henrietta Maria. His diplomatic efforts proved no more tactful than Buckingham's, as he used the occasion to attempt the seduction of Madame de Chevreuse. Accordingly, James Hay, the Earl of Carlisle and the King's former lover, was also despatched to France, to try to rescue the situation.

When James I died, Buckingham found himself in a more powerful position than ever before. Although rumours that he had murdered the old king circulated widely, they could not be substantiated. Toxicology was in its infancy. An ad-hoc post-mortem merely confirmed that James's physical state had already been very poor. His enlarged heart was soft; he was suffering from a host of diseases, including kidney stones, blackened lungs and a brain so swollen that it oozed out when the embalmer began his grisly work.

Charles's first act as King was to clear away the beggars and prostitutes that loitered around the gates of his palace. Then he set about taking himself a wife – though he himself was not present for the actual ceremony in Notre Dame. A French Duke acted as his stand-in.

Charles found it hard to disguise his lack of enthusiasm for the gawky, fifteen-year-old Henrietta Maria. He was not on the quay to greet her when she arrived at Dover and although, when they met, he embraced her and kissed her politely, his disappointment was plain for all to see.

The couple sent their first night together at Lord Wotton's house in Canterbury. Charles took great care to bolt every door and window of the wedding chamber, perhaps expecting the trouble that was to follow. At any event, their nocturnal activities were certainly not to the liking of the inexperienced Henrietta Maria. When they reached London, she declared that she was 'indisposed' and refused to appear in public.

Buckingham tried to help, urging the Queen's lady of the bedchamber, Madame St Georges, to persuade the young woman to be a little more forthcoming in bed. She replied brusquely that she never interfered in those sort of matters and, as a result, Henrietta's entire retinue was sacked. Within six weeks, the King and Queen were living apart and the marriage seemed effectively to be at an end. Despite this, Charles did not seek consolation in the arms of mistresses – not even the beautiful, affectionate and experienced Lady Carlisle, who was admired by all the men in the court and envied by all the women. Thomas, Lord Cromwell, confided to a friend that he could not stop thinking of her, though he added that 'my wife gets something by such thoughts nightly wherein I commit I doubt not adultery'. The poet Sir John Suckling shared these desires and, in one of his verses, he mentally undressed the lady as she took her daily walk in the gardens at Hampton Court.

> *I was undoing all she wore*
> *And had she walked but one turn more*
> *Eve in her first state had not been*
> *So naked or so plainly seen.*

However, it was Buckingham who used his influence to turn these sort of fantasies into reality. He despatched the Earl of Carlise, the former royal favourite James Hay, abroad on a diplomatic mission, so that he could seduce his wife.

When his own wife found out about the affair, Buckingham tried to pass Lady Carlisle on to the King. He declined the offer and, instead, made her a lady of the Queen's bedchamber. Some suspected that this might be a subtle ploy and that Lady Carlilse might train the young Queen in the arts of love. One courtier noted that 'she has already brought her to paint and in time will lead her into more debaucheries'.

The idea worked. When Buckingham was assassinated by a disgruntled naval officer, the royal couple were quickly reconciled and within weeks Henrietta Maria was pregnant. In all, they had nine children, with two more stillborn.

In public, however, the royal couple continued to endorse the notion of chaste courtly love. All the masques and plays that were performed at court were strictly censored. Henry James, who made one of the Queen's maids pregnant and then refused to marry her, was dismissed from his post and Charles refused to commute the death sentence imposed on the Earl of Castlehaven for rape and buggery.

Even the wife of a parliamentarian colonel acknowledged that 'the nobility and courtiers who did not quite abandon their debaucheries had yet that reverence to the King to retire into corners to practise them.'

The air of restraint at the court was not sufficient, however, to appease the growing band of Puritans, who regarded all theatre as a sign of vice. The Queen's acting and recitation, it was generally agreed, surpassed all others', but the complaint was made that at her masques, ladies dressed in 'men's apparel'.

When the Puritan barrister William Prynne wrote that actresses were 'notorious, impudent, prostituted strumpets', Charles took it as an affront to the Queen. Prynne was sentenced to lose both ears in the pillory. This sort of high-handed attitude increased the King's unpopularity and was one of the factors which led to the Civil War and, ultimately, the King's downfall.

At the end of the war, when he was imprisoned on the Isle of Wight, Charles had one last romance with Jane Whorwood, the wife of the royalist leader of the City of London. She had first come to court with half of the £1,000 her husband had raised for the King. In lieu of the other half, Charles kept her as a courtier.

On 26th July 1648, six months before his execution, the doomed monarch wrote to 'Sweet Jane Whorwood' asking her to meet him in his room as if 'by accident'. During his imprisonment, he wrote at least sixteen letters to her and outwitted his guards on numerous occasions, in order to see her.

Their affair was said to be platonic, and Charles said he would tell his wife about her. In the end, he never did. In his last letter to Jane, he wrote that she 'had given him great contentment'. It would have taken a very cold man indeed not to crave the pleasures of the flesh once more before he died – and a very heartless woman to have denied them to him.

5

THE MERRY
MONARCHS

The Restoration court of Charles II was described by the diarist Samual Pepys as 'nothing almost but bawdy from top to bottom'. It could just as easily have been summed up by Charles's personal motto: 'God will never damn a man for allowing himself a little pleasure.'

And allow himself pleasure was precisely what the 'Merry Monarch' did. During the nine years of his enforced exile on the Continent, when England was ruled by Parliament and Oliver Cromwell, Charles went through no fewer than seventeen official mistresses.

At fifteen, he had gained his first experience of that 'little fantastical gentleman called Cupid' when he was seduced by his former wet nurse, Christabella Wyndham, the wife of the royalist governor of Bridgewater. No doubt, this was why the prince's adviser, Edward Hyde, called her 'a woman of great rudeness and country pride'.

A year later, when Charles was on his way to France, he stopped off in Jersey and is said to have seduced Margaret de Carteret, the daughter of a local aristocrat. According to letters found in Jesuit archives, she even bore him a child; Charles's first bastard, it seems, went on to become a priest.

In Paris, Steenie's son, the new Duke of Buckingham, who had spent much time in the promiscuous Italian courts, was on hand to introduce the young prince to the delights of the city. This was clearly much appreciated by Charles.

'During his exile he delivered himself so entirely to his pleasures that he became incapable of application,' said the future Bishop of Salisbury.

In 1649, just three months after his father had been executed, Charles took up with Lucy Walters, a stunning brunette whom the diarist John Evelyn called 'a beautiful strumpet'. Lucy was originally from Wales and had fled to Holland with her lover, the royalist Colonel Sydney. He sold her to his brother, but she did not stay long before moving in with a man called Barlow. When Charles first met her, she was calling herself 'Mrs Barlow'. As a contemporary later remarked about Charles's mistresses: 'Seldom was he possessed of their first favours.'

Charles and Lucy lived together briefly and she bore him a son, James, who was duly created Duke of Monmouth. When Charles went to Scotland to raise support for the royalist cause in 1650–51, he had to leave Lucy behind. This may have been to his benefit. By now, his reputation as a lecher was doing him as much harm in Presbyterian Scotland as it was in Puritan England.

While Charles was away, Lucy took other lovers and had a daughter whom Charles would not acknowledge as his own.

In 1656, Lucy unwisely travelled to England with one of these partners, a Colonel Howard. She was arrested as a royalist spy and, in a propaganda coup, deported as Charles's whore. Charles then seized his son James, but discarded the unreliable Lucy. She died of syphilis and went to a pauper's grave.

All this – at least James, the troublesome Duke of Monmouth – could have been prevented. One of Charles's courtiers in exile was a Colonel Cundum, who is believed to have given his name to the condom. He was possibly responsible for its introduction into Britain. The sheath had been invented more than a century earlier by Gabriel Fallopius, the Italian anatomist who discovered the uterus – the Fallopian tubes are named after him – and was responsible for naming the vagina and the clitoris. The first condoms were made from fish skins and their purpose was not contraception, but protection against syphilis, which had just arrived in Europe and was sweeping the Continent. Before the discovery of penicillin in 1929 and its first medical use in 1941, syphilis was a killer disease and, in the seventeenth century, far more pernicious than AIDS.

Charles had three more royal bastards before returning to England – one by Elizabeth Killigrew and two by the beautiful Catherine Pegge, both daughters of exiled cavaliers. He was also conducting a discreet affair with the twice-widowed Lady Elizabeth Byron. Generally, though, Charles preferred sophisticated Continental women, such as Madame de Chatillon. Charles called her 'Bablon' and their relationship continued for several years without any tiresome arguments about fidelity.

During his travels in Holland, Germany, France and Spain, Charles found many pretty women who were ready to accommodate the wishes of an exiled king. Seventeen of his mistresses are known, but there must have been many other casual affairs. One Cromwellian spy in Charles's retinue painted a vivid picture of 'fornication, drunkenness and adultery'. He even said that the 'great abomination' – going to the theatre on a Sunday was 'esteemed no sin' by the Prince and his cohorts.

Appropriately enough, when the call came for Charles to return to England in 1660, his current lover was an Englishwoman. As a teenager, Barbara Villiers had already established a formidable reputation as a temptress. During her childhood, she was described as 'a little lecherous girl ... [who] used to rub her thing with her fingers or against the end of forms.' By her teens, she had become the mistress of the Earl of Chesterfield. Then, in 1659, she had married a country gentleman called Roger Palmer, while happily continuing her affair with Chesterfield.

Early in the following year, a group of royalist conspirators sent the then Mrs Palmer as an emissary to Charles's exiled court in the Netherlands. He was immediately taken with her dazzling good looks and her predatory sexuality. She was just nineteen – he twenty-nine when they met, and she soon became 'the lewdest as well as the fairest of King Charles's concubines'.

Barbara had studied the banned sonnets of Pietro Aretin, whose work graphically illustrated the sixteen sexual positions then known to mankind. Indeed, Sir Thomas Carew said she 'hath all the tricks of Aretin that are to be practised to give pleasure.' The expertise gave her an edge over her rivals and Charles rapidly embraced his new lover with true patriotic zeal. By the time that he was proclaimed King in May 1660, Barbara had become his regular partner in the royal bedchamber. It was even said that Charles II celebrated his first night back in London in the arms of Barbara Palmer, siring their first child.

Samuel Pepys quickly fell under her spell, too, 'tho' I know she is a whore'. However, when he saw her petticoats hanging out to dry, he exclaimed that her lingerie was the finest 'I ever saw, and it did me much good to look at them'. He later wrote that he had dreamed about sleeping with her – 'My Lady Castlemaine [as she was to become] in my arms, and was admitted to use all the dalliance I desired with her.' This dream, Pepys declared was 'the best that was ever dreamed'.

Barbara Palmer does not seem to have been conspicuously faithful to Charles. The Bishop of Salisbury claimed that she was 'most vicious and ravenous; foolish but imperious, very uneasy to the King, and always carrying on intrigues with other men.' She slept with the Earl of St Albans and Miss Hobart, who was another of the King's lovers.

Barbara Palmer had returned to England as the *maîtresse en tître*, but the convention-bound English establishment would not recognise her position. The Lord Chancellor, Edward Hyde, refused to seal any document that bore her name.

In February 1661, nine months after the Restoration, she gave birth to a daughter. Gossips ascribed paternity of the child to the King, to Chesterfield or even – very occasionally – to her husband. Later that year, Palmer was created Earl of Castlemaine – 'the reason whereof everyone knows,' wrote Samuel Pepys. This also provided his wife – and any children – with a title. Lady Castlemaine was soon pregnant once more. This time there was no doubt that the father was the King, who was soon known throughout the land as 'Old Rowley' after the goat that was tethered on the palace green. Lewd jokes and earthy verses compared the King's sexual prowess favourably with the appetite and stamina of the old goat. In all, Lady Castlemaine produced three sons and two daughters who were acknowledged by the King.

Fortunately for Charles, her fertility did not diminish her desires. Even in advanced pregnancy she would gladly receive a suppertime visit from him. During their eight years together, she amassed a huge fortune and all her children were ennobled.

But for a King, a concubine was not enough. He had to have a wife, so that he could sire legitimate heirs. Ever willing, Lady Castlemaine helped him choose. The list she drew up was not guaranteed to excite his passions. Charles rejected the Prince of Parma's oldest daughter because she was too ugly and the youngest because she was too crude. Similarly the legions of available German princesses were dismissed because they were 'all dull and foggy'.

Eventually, he accepted Catherine of Braganza, the King of Portugal's daughter, largely because she brought with her a dowry of £360,000, along with naval bases in Tangiers and Bombay, and lucrative trading privileges in South America. He might have had second thoughts if he had seen her first. When she arrived in England, she had her hair dressed in the Portuguese fashion, with corkscrew braids sticking out on either side of her head. 'I thought they had brought me a bat instead of a woman,' he confided to a friend.

Catherine was no less thrilled. When she heard that she was to be married to the King of England, a practising protestant, she made a special pilgrimage to the shrine of a saint. She also promised her mother that she would banish Charles's lovers. One of Charles's courtiers described her as an 'ill natured little goblin, and designed for nothing but to dance and vex mankind'.

Charles had been brought up to be civil to women, especially great ones, so he kept his feelings to himself. They were wed in Portsmouth in 1662. After a disappointing wedding night, Charles treated his bride so kindly that some thought the marriage might actually prosper – 'which I fear will put Madame Castlemaine's nose out of joint,' wrote Samuel Pepys.

But neither Catherine nor the diarist knew the true score. For Charles had also made a promise to Lady Castlemaine – namely that she would become a Lady of the Bedchamber.

When Lady Castlemaine was presented to the Queen, the sniggers of the courtiers alerted her to the situation. She immediately fainted, complaining of a nose bleed. For weeks, Catherine and Charles argued over 'the Lady'. Finally, the Queen gave in. She befriended Barbara in the hope that her generosity would shame Charles into continuing his visits to her chamber. The King had many more enticing prospects than the Queen but he 'kept her for breeding' as one cynic put it.

While Lady Castlemaine was embarrassingly fecund, Catherine of Braganza never gave birth to an heir. And while government ministers advised Charles to divorce her and take another wife to secure the royal line, Charles never abandoned his wife. She, in turn, grew to accept her husband's mistresses. She would rarely visit his chambers uninvited in case she caught him with another woman. Once she discovered a lady's slipper under his bed and withdrew, laughing, so that 'the pretty fool' could come out of hiding.

The year after his marriage, Charles fell in love with fifteen-year-old Frances Stuart. She was described by one contemporary as 'the prettiest girl in the world and the most fitted to adorn a court'. Even a lofty French intellectual conceded: 'It was hardly possible for a woman to have less wit or more beauty.' Her beauty was immortalised on British coinage for centuries – she was the model for Britannia on the pre-decimal penny piece.

Soon, the King was 'kissing her to the observation of all the world,' but Frances refused to let him 'do anything more than is safe to her'. Her resistance only inflamed his ardour. His friends set up a 'committee for the getting of Mistress Stuart for the King'. If Catherine of Braganza were to die, it was said, the King would marry Frances. They even staged a 'mock marriage' complete with ceremonial bedding. But Lady Castlemaine, who had already enjoyed affairs with several courtiers – Cavendish, Henningham, Scrope and the King's bastard son Monmouth – knew how to handle the situation. She invited Frances to sleep with her and then flaunted the fact that she had succeeded where the King had failed.

Lady Castlemaine managed to maintain her position by keeping a 'stable' of young women for Charles's pleasure. She also secured advancement for her own lovers. One former beau, Thomas Wood, was made Bishop of Coventry. Among her other admirers were the Duke of Buckingham, the playwright William Wycherley and Henry Jermyn, the future Lord Dover. She also seduced the young John Churchill, later the Duke of Marlborough, who was said at the time to be 'a youth of most beautiful form and graceful aspect'. The King once caught them in *flagrante delicto* and said to the penniless Churchill: 'I forgive you, for you do it for your bread.'

The rakish poet Rochester summed up her reputation in a few witty lines:

> *When she has jaded quite*
> *Her almost boundless appetite . . .*
> *She'll still drudge on in tasteless vice*
> *As if she sinn'd for exercise.*

But Barbara went too far when she seduced Jacob Hall, a tightrope walker, in his booth at St Bartholomew's Fair, followed by a footman in her bath, and then demanded that Charles acknowledge paternity of the resulting child. Indeed, her reputation grew so notorious that one anonymous wit wrote *A Petition of the Poor Whores to the Most Splendid, Illustrious, Serene and Eminent Lady of Pleasure, the Countess of Castlemaine* asking for her support for 'a trade wherein your Ladyship has great experience'. Barbara was livid, but that did not prevent another scribe from penning a mock Gracious Answer on her behalf. Barbara was eventually paid off with a handsome estate close to the palace and was created Duchess of Cleveland.

Some contrasted her fortunes to those of Jane Shore, the mistress of Edward IV, who was punished rather than paid for her promiscuity. 'The reason why she is not duck'd, Because by Caesar she is fucked,' ran a couplet pinned to her door. A reward of £1,000 was offered for the name of the author, but no one dared to claim it.

'Madam,' said Charles to Lady Castlemaine on their parting, 'all I ask of you for your own sake is to live so in future as to make the least noise you can, and I care not who you love.'

Which was just as well, as Lady Castlemaine swiftly took a succession of new lovers. Once again, Rochester provided a pithy commentary:

> Castlemaine I say is much to be admir'd,
> Although she ne'er was satisfied or tired,
> Full forty men a day provided for this whore,
> Yet like a bitch, she wags her tail for more.

Unfortunately, Barbara's escapades were not as discreet as the King had wished. Her affair with the English Ambassador in Paris caused a political scandal. She eventually lost her fortune when a young man, 'Beau' Fielding, bigamously married her when she was sixty-four.

The King, meanwhile, remained addicted to women. 'Lady Middleton, Lady Denham, the Queen's and the duchess's maids of honour, and a hundred others bestow their favours right and left, and not the least notice is taken of their conduct,' wrote one courtier, barely concealing his envy. The clergy were more critical: 'He usually came from his mistress's lodgings to church, even on sacrament days,' noted one disgruntled cleric.

The mistresses included the Countess of Kildare; Lady Falmouth, who later took up with Charles's brother, the Duke of York; Jane Roberts, a clergyman's daughter who later became the mistress of the Earl of Rochester, then died repenting her adulteries; and Winifred Wells, who was said to have 'the carriage of a goddess and the physiognomy of a dreamy sheep'.

It was said of Winifred that she came from a loyal family and that 'her father having faithfully served Charles I, she thought it her duty not to revolt against Charles II.' According to one fanciful tale, she suffered a miscarriage of her royal child during a court ball, but recovered sufficiently to dance on, leaving the foetus on the floor.

There were scores of other nameless ladies, whom the Keeper of the Closet, William Chaffinch, would escort to the King's bedchamber whenever Charles was in London, or across the road from the Maiden Inn, when he was at his country house in Newmarket.

The Earl of Rochester, as always, was swift to suggest the reason for the King's popularity:

> *Nor are his high Desires above his strength.*
> *His Sceptre and his prick are a length,*
> *And she may sway the one who plays with the other,*
> *And makes him little wiser than his brother.*

The brother in question was the profligate James, Duke of York.

The King also looked outside the court for his sport. He soon became interested in the new breed of actresses. Charles had restored the theatre, banned under Cromwell, and women were allowed for the first time to appear on the stage. This outraged the remaining puritans, who argued that actresses were no better than prostitutes.

Moll Davis was one of the first to come to Charles's attention, while playing the guitar and singing 'My Lodging It is on the Cold Ground.' This prompted the Queen to leave the room, allowing the King to raise 'the fair songstress from the cold ground to the bed royal,' as the contemporary wit John Downes wrote. Soon her lodging was a £600 house in Suffolk Street which Charles had bought for her. Moll was known for her sensuous lips and Pepys dubbed her 'the most impertinent slut in the world'. She had a daughter by Charles – Lady Mary Tudor – and when the King tired of her, she returned to the stage.

Nell Gwyn, one of Moll's friends, was the cause of the rift between them. She was heartily sick of the airs and graces that Moll had adopted and so decided to doctor her sweetmeats. When the King went around that night for a romantic assignation, he found Moll prostrate with diarrhoea. Nell then stepped in to render the services that her colleague was unable to provide.

'Pretty, witty Nell' came from a humble background. Her father died in Oxford jail and her mother sold ale in Mrs Ross's brothel in Drury Lane. 'I was brought up in a bawdy house to fill strong waters to the guests,' Nell admitted. Rochester thought her duties extended further. He wrote that she was: 'By Madam Ross exposed to town I mean to those who will give half-a-crown.' Two shillings and sixpence was the going rate for a prostitute at the time. Indeed, when her sister was arrested for prostitution, Nell pleaded her case by saying: 'Twas surely a pity and a waste to let a young whore scarred with neither the pox nor infected with the clap to languish in prison.'

Nell was good looking, with long slender legs, generous breasts and a mouth 'that makes mine water at it'. Although she was illiterate, she had a sharp wit and soon attracted a string of lovers, among them, apparently, the poet John Dryden. Nell later joked to the King that when he got married it had broken her heart and left her with no reason to preserve her virginity.

She worked selling oranges outside the King's Theatre and soon became the mistress of the actor Charles Hart, the great-nephew of Shakespeare. Nell mischievously dubbed him Charles the First. He put her on the stage and she rapidly became one of the Theatre Royal's leading actresses. Charles Sackville, Lord Buckhurst, became her next lover, earning him the nickname of Charles the Second. Buckhurst was notorious for appearing naked when preaching from the balcony of Kate's Tavern in Covent Garden. In due course, Charles II became 'Charles the Third'.

He had seen her many times on the stage, before she usurped the position of Moll Davis. Charles particularly liked it when she appeared dressed in men's clothing, and even paid for a costume that would fly up and reveal her legs. Nell was soon 'the indiscreetest and wildest creature that was ever in a court'. Nonetheless, she remained faithful to Charles. 'I am but one man's whore,' she said. Even so, her services were expensive. She initially asked for £500 a year, but in four years she extracted more than £60,000 out of her royal admirer. One of the things she spent the money on was an erotic silver bedstead, which was the talk of London. On it there were depictions of tightrope-walker Jacob Hall mounting Lady Castlemaine and another of the King's mistresses, Louise de Keroualle, lying in a tomb with a dusky Eastern potentate.

She never received a title. He 'never treated her with the decencies of a mistress but rather with the lewdness of a prostitute,' said Bishop Burnet. Charles traditionally gave his mistresses the title of 'duchess'. Nell was well aware of this and when, on one occasion Charles complimented her on a new dress saying 'You are fine enough to be a queen,' Nell's witty riposte was: 'And whore enough to be a duchess.' Nevertheless, she did manage to secure titles for their sons – her 'little bastards' as she would call them in the King's presence.

Some courtiers considered Nell well worth the money the King squandered on her because she never meddled in serious matters. 'She hath got a trick to handle his prick, but never lay hands upon his sceptre,' wrote Rochester. When asked for her advice by the King she 'told his Majestie to lock up his codpiece,' one chronicler claimed. She never interceded for politicians and 'never broke into those amorous infidelities which others are accused of'. Indeed, when Buckingham 'fumbled' her and was not discouraged by a slap, Nell reported his behaviour to the King.

Some, of course, were shocked by the openness of the affair. The diarist John Evelyn reported walking in St James's Park, near the house Charles had given Nell in Pall Mall, and hearing the King and his mistress in 'very familiar discourse' over the garden wall. An alderman in

Newmarket was equally scandalised when Nell asked in public 'Charles, I hope I shall have your company at night shall I not?'

She also made no secret of her belief that she should have the freehold of the house in Pall Mall because she always 'offered her services free under the Crown'.

Although Nell Gwyn was faithful to Charles, he did not return the compliment. For much of the time, she had to share him with a beautiful Breton girl called Louise de Keroualle, while the French ambassador was convinced that the only woman who had a real hold on him was his sister.

Fourteen years his junior, Henrietta-Anne had always been Charles's favourite relation. He called her 'Min ette' and wrote her long letters, revealing his innermost thoughts and even describing the intimate details of his wedding night.

Henrietta-Anne had been married in her mid-teens to the King of France's younger brother Philippe, Duke of Orleans. He was a homosexual and a transvestite, who loved to totter about in high-heeled shoes wearing perfume and rouge. He also had violent tendencies and was pathologically possessive with his wife. So she was genuinely worried about the consequences when King Louis propositioned her. Wisely, she evaded the potentially lethal caresses of the King by sending her maid-of-honour, Louisa de la Vallière, to the assignation in her place.

In 1670, Henrietta-Anne came to England to visit her brother, bringing with her the young Louise de Keroualle as her maid. Charles was smitten and begged his sister to leave her behind, but Henrietta-Anne refused, saying that she had promised Louise's parents that she would bring her home safely.

Three weeks later Henrietta-Anne died and Charles was devastated. Louis XIV was quick to exploit the situation. Thinking it would do no harm to have an agent in the King of England's bed, he arranged for Louise to return to England as maid of honour to Queen Catherine.

At first Louise clung stubbornly to her virginity, but the French ambassador eventually persuaded her to sacrifice her honour for her country. She may have hoped to become Charles's wife and made frequent enquiries about the Queen's health. However, after a 'mock marriage' at Euston Hall in October 1672, she finally succumbed. 'The fair lady was bedded one of these nights,' recorded John Evelyn, 'and the stocking flung after the manner of a married bride.' This referred to the custom of throwing stockings to courtiers waiting outside the nuptial bedchamber to symbolize the consummation of the union.

There was, in this instance, no doubt about the reality of the consummation. Nine months later Louis XIV sent his congratulations on a mission well done. Louise was created Duchess of Portsmouth and lady of the Queen's bedchamber, 'to rank as high as any of the older mistresses who were Duchesses'.

Charles called her 'my dear life' and said 'I love you better than all the world besides.' She was said to be 'wondrous handsome' even though she had a slight cast in one eye. With her typically earthy sense of humour Nell Gwyn called her 'Squintabella,' until she noticed Louise's tendency to feign illness and burst into tears at the slightest excuse. Then Nell dubbed her 'The Weeping Willow'.

Nell reacted mischievously to Louise's snobbery, and her claims to be descended from a long line of aristocrats. 'If she be such a lady of quality,' Nell enquired, 'why does she demean herself to be a courtesan?' Similarly, after Louise appeared in mourning over some supposed aristocratic cousin, Nell donned weeds the next day. 'Have you not heard,' she said, 'of the death of the Cham of Tartary?'

As well as the lands and jewels Charles lavished on her, Louise received handsome gifts from the French. 'Why is it', Nell asked the French ambassador, 'that the King of France does not send presents to me, instead of the Weeping Willow?'

The English people thought they knew the answer. Above the door of Louise's sumptuous apartments in the recently refurbished Palace of Whitehall appeared the sign:

> *Within this place a bed's appointed*
> *For a French bitch and God's annointed.*

There were even threats against her life. One day a coach approached the royal apartments with a pretty young woman inside it. Thinking this was Louise de Keroualle, a noisy mob surrounded it, shouting anti-Catholic abuse. But it was Nell Gwyn who stuck her head out of the window. 'Pray good people be civil, I am the Protestant whore,' she cried, turning the jeers into laughter.

In 1675, Hortense de Mancini, the Duchess of Mazarin, arrived in England. During his exile, Charles had enjoyed a passionate affair with her and there had even been talk of marriage. In her early twenties, she had been an extraordinary beauty, with a mystique that many men found irresistible. She had married, but her first husband, the Duke of Mazarin, was a religious fanatic, who forced her to perform the most elaborate penances for all her sins, real or imagined. So she disguised herself as a boy and ran away from him after five years, becoming instead the mistress of the Duke of Savoy. When he died, his widow strongly advised her to leave the area and Hortense moved to England, with her pet parrot and a black page-boy named Mustapha, 'befeathered and bewigged' and wearing trousers. Despite this strange retinue, the French ambassador remarked that he had never seen 'anyone who so well defies the power of time and vice to disfigure'.

The King's youthful passion was swiftly rekindled. 'Madame Mazarin is well satisfied with the conversation she had had with the King of England,' reported the French envoy and, indeed, Charles immediately installed her in Lady Castlemaine's old apartments. The arrival of another foreign mistress did not, however, meet with universal approval, as one contemporary complained:

> *That the king should send of another French whore*
> *When one already had made him poor.*

Nell Gwyn, in contrast, was delighted. She donned black robes and staged a mock funeral for Louise's dead aspirations. A ballad from the time ran:

> *Since Cleveland is fled till she's brought to bed,*

THE MERRY MONARCHS

And Nelly is quite forgotten,
And Mazarin is as old as the Queen,
And Portsmouth, the young whore, is rotten.

The affair with Hortense was intense but short-lived. The King was growing old and Hortense was too demanding. 'Each sex provides its lovers for Hortense,' observed one courtier and when the young Prince of Monaco turned up in London, it soon became evident that Hortense had found herself a new lover.

Louise, too, had cast her net elsewhere. The King caught her in the act with her new admirer – 'coming himself a little abruptly on them, he saw more than he himself had a mind to see.'

Charles soon realized that Louise meant more to him than any of his other lovers. 'After this the King kissed her often before all the world, which he was never observed to do before this time,' wrote Bishop Burnet. However, he still spent the afternoons with Hortense and the evenings with his dear Nell.

Despite their obvious rivalry, the three women got on well with each other, sharing a common interest in gambling. In a single afternoon, Hortense is said to have won £5,000 from Nell and £8,000 from Louise. The fastidious Nell used to complain that the other two women were dirty. She told the French ambassador that Louise's underwear was foul and that Hortense wore none. To emphasize her point, she lifted her own skirts for the ambassador to carry out his personal inspection. Her petticoats were indeed very clean.

Louise bedded the Moroccan ambassador, while Hortense took on a number of lovers. When one of them was killed in a duel, however, she threatened to become a

89

nun – a prospect that greatly amused the King. Only Nell remained faithful.

On 31st January 1685, John Evelyn took a last look at Charles's court and wrote: 'I am never to forget the unexpressible luxury and profaneness, gaming and all dissolution and, as it were, total forgetfulness of God (it being Sunday evening) which ... I was witness of: the King sitting and toying with his concubines, Portsmouth, Cleveland and Mazarin, etc; whilst about twenty courtiers and other dissolute persons were at basset [a gambling game] round a large table, a bank of at least two thousand in gold before them, upon which two gentlemen that were with me made reflections with astonishment, it being a scene of utmost vanity, and surely, as they thought, would never have an end. Six days after, all was dust.'

On 6th February 1685, Charles died. On his deathbed he begged his brother James to 'let not poor Nelly starve'. He also predicted, rightly as it turned out, that his brother would 'lose his kingdom by his bigotry and his soul for a lot of trollops'. The King was critical because, unlike himself, James went with 'unsightly wantons'.

Despite catching venereal disease from Charles, Louise survived for another fifty years. She bought a small estate in France, but the rest of her wealth was squandered. James II gave her a small pension and, later on, Louis XIV helped out. She was given a grant 'in consideration of the great service she has rendered to France' from the Regent of Orleans, who was renowned for consorting with a hundred mistresses of unsurpassed ugliness. When scolded about this by his mother, he replied: 'Bah, in the night all cats are grey.'

Nell did not starve, though her creditors almost landed her in a debtors' prison. James came to her rescue. Even though she was still a young woman, she only survived two years after the death of Charles II and never took another lover. She turned down one hopeful young suitor by saying that she would not 'lay a dog where the deer had laid'.

Of the 26 dukes in England today, five are direct descendants of Charles II and his mistresses. His extramarital activities were also responsible for several marquises and earls.

Although Charles II was undoubtedly a shameless womanizer, even his exploits paled beside those of his brother James. Charles once told the French ambassador: 'I do not believe there are two men who love women more than you and I do, but my brother, devout as he is, loves them more.'

Charles's young brother James, the Duke of York and later James II, escaped from Carisbrooke Castle during the Civil War dressed as a girl. Abroad, he shared the King's libidinous habits, but unlike his brother, James appeared more interested in quantity than quality, and Charles suggested that his ugly mistresses were, in fact, penances imposed on him by the priest for the good of his soul.

During his long exile, James had tried to negotiate marriage with the heiress of the Duc de Longueville. When that failed, he secretly married Anne Hyde, the daughter of Charles's prudish Lord Chancellor, who had served as maid of honour to his own sister Mary. Anne was already carrying James's child when the family returned to England at the Restoration. James then went through a conventional wedding ceremony in England, in an effort to legitimize his pregnant wife's position. Chronicling the event, Samuel Pepys recorded a remark made by the Earl of Sandwich: 'That he that doth get a wench with child and marries her afterward, it is as if a man should shit in his hat and then clap it upon his head.'

When her father, the strait-laced Lord Chancellor, heard of the scandal, he demanded that his daughter should be taken to the Tower of London immediately to await execution. James, meanwhile, insisted that, unless Anne was officially acknowledged as his wife, he would leave the kingdom and spend the rest of his life abroad.

His situation was complicated when Charles I's widow, Henrietta-Maria, and her daughter Mary, who was then the Princess of Orange, both expressed outrage at the marriage. Mary declared that she would never accept as her sister-in-law a former maid of honour who had once 'stood as a servant behind her chair'. Both Mary and Henrietta-Maria rushed over from the continent, intent on preventing 'so great a stain and dishonour on the Crown'.

Faced with this family split, James himself began to waver. Anne's plain looks and dumpy figure had not been enhanced by her pregnancy, and he began to pursue instead the many young beauties who had flocked to the Restoration court. At the same time, five of his friends obligingly claimed to be the father of Anne's child. One of them, Harry Killigrew, said that 'he had found the critical minute in a certain closet built over water for a purpose very different from that of giving ease to the pains of love.' This water closet was the scene of many assignations, he alleged. Another self-styled lover, Sir Charles Berkeley, offered to marry Anne to save James from a wife who was 'so wholly unworthy of him'. To cap it all, James himself denied that he had ever married the woman.

On 22nd October 1660, Anne gave birth to a sickly boy. Throughout her pregnancy, she doggedly maintained that James was her husband and the father of her child. At length, the King took pity on her. He quelled the scandal by insisting that James 'must drink as he had brewed and live with her who he had made his wife.' The Duke's five friends were forced to retract their allegations and on 21st December 1660 James publicly admitted the marriage. Three days latch, Princess Mary died of smallpox, expressing regret for the things she had said about her former maid of honour. Only the Queen Mother, Henrietta-Maria, remained obdurate. If Anne was ever brought to the palace at Whitehall, she said, she would leave by another door and never come back. But even she was, eventually, forced to accept the marriage. On 1st January 1661, she consented to receive Anne, saying that she had always liked her from the beginning. The disastrous split in the royal family had thus been mended, leaving James and Charles free to continue in their lascivious ways.

James quickly established a reputation as 'the most unguarded ogler of his time'. Though married, he 'thought that he was entitled . . . to give way to a little inconstancy'.

'He hath come out of his wife's bed, and gone to others laid in bed for him,' wrote Pepys. The diarist took a special interest in the affairs of the Duke of York who, as the Lord High Admiral, was also his employer.

Anne's response to her husband's philandering was to eat excessively. Her figure ballooned, but by now James was aware that she had 'wit and other qualities capable of surprising a heart less inclinable to sex than was that of his Royal Highness in the first warmth of his youth'.

She made a good consort, giving birth to two healthy children – Anne and Mary – who both went on to become Queens. Six other babies were stillborn. James also asked her for her advice. Pepys related how 'the Duke of York in all things but his codpiece is led by his wife'.

Even so, Charles still made a habit of seducing his wife's maids of honour and securing positions in her bedchamber for his mistresses. These privileges, however, were scant reward for the ever-present risk of pregnancy.

Miss Trevor, 'the prettiest of the Duchess's maids of honour', was obliged to run away from court. 'Had she stayed much longer she had been delivered at St James.' The mother of Sarah Jennings tried to drag her daughter home, on the grounds that 'two of the maids of honour had had great bellies at court and she would not leave her child there to have the third.'

Lord Roberts whisked his wife back to her country home, rather than risk her being seduced by the Duke. Denied these favours, James 'immediately seized upon whatever he could first lay his hands upon; this was Lady Carnegy, who had been in several hands.'

Pepys claimed that the latter's husband 'did get out of her that she did dishonour him and so bid her to continue.' He then deliberately contracted venereal disease in the hope of passing this on to the Duke.

Once Lord Chesterfield saw James fondling his wife while the Queen played cards. When the Duke realized he had been spotted, he 'almost undressed my lady in pulling away his hand'.

Pepys had heard that the Duke was 'smitten in love with my Lady Chesterfield' and was scarcely surprised when he witnessed the Duke and Duchess of York out together, even though the former had just come from 'kissing and leaning upon another'.

When Lord Chesterfield realized what was going on, he took his wife away from London. James immediately turned his attention to Lady Falmouth, then to Mary Kirke – only to find that she was also entertaining his nephew Monmouth. Next, there came Jane Middleton, who carried 'about her body a continual base smell, that is very offensive, especially if she were hote.' Personal hygiene was still not regarded as a priority.

After a brief fling with the 'small and stumpy' Godotha Price, another of his wife's maids of honour, James took up with pretty Lady Elizabeth Denham, the wife of a royal poet. Sir John Denham was fifty and his young wife was eighteen. At first, the poet agreed to collude in their affair, provided that his wife was given a position in the Duchess's household. However, Elizabeth was not content to be a secret mistress, furtively climbing up and down the Privy Stairs, but was anxious to be publicly acknowledged. Soon, 'this bitch Denham' was being followed around 'like a dog' by James on public occasions.

Pepys often complained that his master, the Lord High Admiral 'is gone over to all his pleasures again, and leaves off care of business, what with his woman, my Lady Denham, and his hunting three times a week'.

Sir John Denham became extremely piqued at the very public nature of his cuckolding. The couple conducted their assignations openly at his house in Scotland Yard. One day he caught them together, giggling over a guitar. In a rage, he grabbed the instrument and smashed it to the ground. He then complained about the Duke of York's conduct to the King – much to Charles's amusement, no doubt.

The affair only ended with Lady Denham's sudden death. Poison was suspected and the only way the poet could prevent his neighbours tearing him limb from limb at the funeral was by plying them with very large quantities of wine. The Duke of York vowed never to 'have another public mistress again'.

He did not keep these good intentions for long. Even before the death of Lady Denham, he had taken up with Arabella Churchill, yet another of the Duchess's maids of honour. No one could understand the attraction of the spindly Arabella. 'That ugly skeleton Churchill' was 'a tall creature, pale-faced, and nothing but skin and bone.' However, the Duke had seen her fall off a horse, revealing a slender pair of legs, and 'could hardly believe that limbs of such exquisite beauty should belong to Miss Churchill's face.' The legs were soon parted and Arabella had to retire to France to give birth to her first royal bastard, James Fitzjames.

Eventually, she bore him four children, ignoring the advice of the King's physician and court abortionist, Alexander Fraser, who was known among the ladies of the court for his skill 'in helping them slip their calves when there is the occasion'.

But that did not stop James. While his wife grew fatter, the Duke of York 'exhausted himself with his inconstancy and was gradually wasting away'.

Anne died six weeks after delivering her final baby. There was talk of poison, but nothing came of it and the Duke soon consoled himself with seventeen-year-old Lady Bellasye. The subject of marriage was mooted, but the King put his foot down.

'It was too much that he had played the fool once; that was not to be done a second time, and at such an age,' he announced. James, by now, was forty.

Instead, the Duke followed his brother's advice and married a foreign princess, Mary of Modena. She was a rare beauty and just fifteen. She was also a Catholic and so pious that she cherished hopes of becoming a nun. It took the intercession of the pope to convince her that wedding the heir to the English throne was a higher calling. Even so, the couple had to be married by proxy, to deflect the anti-Catholic feelings that prevailed in England.

Despite Mary's extraordinary good looks, James was back with Arabella within a week. She produced another healthy child for him, but the Duke of York then abandoned her in favour of Catherine Sedley – this time one of Mary's maids of honour – and Arabella married a colonel, remaining with him for forty years.

The beautiful but promiscuous Catherine was the daughter of a Kentish country gentleman, whose constant infidelity had driven his wife to leave him and incarcerate herself in a nunnery. According to Sir Carr Scopes, Catherine was 'as mad as her mother and as vicious as her father'.

Pepys found her 'none of the most virtuous, but a wit'. Evidence of this latter quality can be found in Catherine's own assessment of her allure for the Duke: 'It cannot be for my beauty, for he must see I have none, and it cannot be my wit, for he has not enough to know I have any.'

Catherine quickly produced a daughter, while Mary was barren. This made her 'very melancholy' and when James finally came to the throne, Mary insisted that he get rid of Catherine, the newly-created Countess of Dorchester. Otherwise, Mary threatened, she would cause a scandal by becoming a nun. Catherine's riposte was that, under the 'Magna Carta', it was the right of every free-born Englishwoman to sleep with her King. A £10,000 mansion and a £4,000 pension persuaded her that this had not been the intention of King John and his barons.

Charles II's bastard son, the Duke of Monmouth, had also inherited his father's love of women. In his time, he pursued several ladies-in-waiting and one of them, Eleanor Needham, gave him four children. But Monmouth raised an army against James. The rebellion was swiftly crushed and Monmouth himself, charged with treason, ended his life on the scaffold. The famous executioner, Jack Ketch, made a mess of the job, requiring five swipes of the axe to dispatch the prisoner. Even then, Monmouth's head was not completely severed and Ketch had to detach it with his knife. At the 'Bloody Assizes', Judge Jeffreys sentenced 320 of Monmouth's followers to be hanged, drawn and quartered, 800 to be transported to Barbados, and hundreds more to be flogged. 'Thus ended this quondam Duke,' wrote John Evelyn, 'darling of his father and the ladies . . . of an easy nature, debauched by lust, seduc'd by crafty knaves.'

Catherine Sedley had been sent to Ireland, but she found it dull. The Irish were 'not only a senseless but a melancholy sort of people,' she told a friend. A year later, she returned to London and James quickly succumbed to her charms once more. In the interim, a miracle had happened. Queen Mary, who was thought to be barren, had given birth to a child.

But this happy news was overshadowed by James's decision to convert to Catholicism; a move that prompted the Bishop of Salisbury to enquire if he had seduced a nun. His conversion meant that the royal heir would be a Catholic. This was more than the protestant lords could stand. They now claimed that the child was illegitimate. During her pregnancy they argued, Mary had padded her belly and had refused to undress in front of the ladies of the bedchamber. The baby, they deduced, had been smuggled into the Queen's bed in a warming pan.

There was, of course, not a shred of truth in this. Twenty ladies of the court, along with numerous high-ranking gentlemen had witnessed the birth, fulfilling the constitutional requirement that persisted up until the birth of Princess Margaret.

James's daughter from his first marriage, Princess Anne, now turned against him and an investigative council was convened which resulted in 'a long discourse of bawdry . . . that put all the ladies to blush'.

The evidence for the legitimacy of the child was strong, particularly as Charles II's former mistress, the Duchess of Mazarin, another Catholic, testified that she had felt the baby in the Queen's stomach during pregnancy. But the prospect that the heir might be genuine only inflamed anti-Catholic feelings still further.

Seven leading opponents of the King invited James's oldest daughter Mary and her protestant husband, William of Orange, to bring an army over to England. James fled, only to return with an army which was defeated at the Battle of the Boyne.

James saw this as punishment for his wicked ways. 'With shame and confusion, I let myself go too much to the love of women which for too long got the better of me: I have paid dearly for it,' he wrote.

He spent his remaining years ruing his mistakes. 'I abhor and detest myself for having ... lived so many years in an almost perpetual course of sin,' he told the Prince of Wales. 'Nothing is more fatal to men, and to great men, than the letting themselves go in the forbidden love of women.'

Despite these lectures, James was as dissolute as ever. One writer mentioned how he had two 'frightful scarecrows' in his train, although he did also spend time with the monks at La Trapp who dressed in winding sheets, contemplated in front of open graves and greeted each other with the cheery salute: 'We must die brothers, we must die.'

'These are the only people I envy,' James said shortly before his own death in 1701. James II certainly lived up to the nickname Nell Gwyn had given him years earlier when she dubbed him 'Dismal Jimmy'.

Although James and his family had fled abroad, his mistress Catherine Sedley, Countess of Dorchester, stayed behind in England. Indeed her father became one of the staunchest supporters of the new regime 'I am even with King James in point of civility,' he said. 'He made my daughter a countess ... I have helped make his daughter a queen.'

Catherine received a pension from William – for acting as a double agent against James – and was also received at court. There, however, she was scorned by the new Queen, James's daughter Mary. Catherine's response was direct: 'Remember Ma'am, if I broke one commandment with your father, you have broken another against him.'

'Both Kings were civil to her,' it was said, but 'both Queens used her badly.'

When she was nearly forty, Catherine married a respectable officer in William's army and eventually bore him two boys. 'If anybody call either of you the son of a whore,' she told them, 'you must bear it, for you are so; but if they call you bastards, fight till you die, for you are an honest man's son.'

This was not quite the end of the Stuarts. James Francis Edward, known as the 'Old Pretender', married Maria Clementina Sobieska, a Polish woman who taught their son, Bonnie Prince Charlie, to treat women with diffidence and cold chivalry, while her husband settled into the debauchery of the Italian courts. The youngster did not learn his mother's lesson well. He cruelly mistreated his Polish mistress, the Princesse de Talmond, though from the accounts of their very public brawls she was more than a match for him.

In Scotland in 1745, he met Clementina Walkinshaw, who bore him a daughter and followed him back into exile. He beat her, too, and his advisers warned him that she was an English spy. In fact, Clementina stayed with him for fifteen years, while he squandered his meagre resources on other mistresses.

Finally, in 1760, she fled, taking refuge in a convent. Charles demanded that Louis XV should force her to come back to him, but the French King took pity on her and refused.

At fifty-one, Charles married. His beautiful nineteen-year-old bride, Princess Louise of Stolberg-Gedern, was dazzled by the prospect of marrying the 'Young Pretender', the tragic hero of the '45 Rebellion and the heir to the English throne. Instead, she found herself saddled with a fat and ageing alcoholic. As a result, she took up with a young Italian poet, Vittorio Alfieri. Charles became jealous and possessive. Normally they slept apart, but one night, in an alcoholic rage, he beat down her bedroom door and raped her. Only the intervention of the servants prevented him from killing her.

Louise escaped to a nunnery and appealed to the pope for protection. When the scandal died down, she and Alfieri lived happily together for the next twenty years.

6

ORANGES ARE NOT THE ONLY FRUIT

William of Orange's father died before the birth of his son, and the child was brought up by an overbearing mother and grandmother. His youth was overshadowed by war. As a result, he spent much time in the company of soldiers and generally preferred the company of men.

William's closest adviser was Hans Willem Bentinck, his former page-boy. William believed that the latter had saved his life. When, as a child, he had been suffering from the smallpox, the page had slept in his bed, 'drawing the fever into himself'. This act of bravery and kindness earned William's undying affection and secured his career.

Throughout William's life, there were rumours that he was a homosexual, though there were certainly several heterosexual episodes. When William was twenty, he visited England. One night, his uncle, Charles II, got him drunk and assailed the apartments of the maids of honour. They were, it was said, 'timely rescued'. There was also talk of an affair with an innkeeper's daughter.

Bishop Burnet said of William: 'He had no vice but of one sort, in which he was very cautious and secret.' The satirist Jonathan Swift, a friend of William's long-standing mistress Elizabeth Villiers, believed that this taste for secrecy lent further weight to the theory that William was indeed a homosexual.

If this was so, William was fortunate indeed in finding a wife who was a lesbian. Both Mary and Anne were brought up with several girl companions in the all-female household at Richmond Palace. The only man they saw regularly before they married was their dissolute half-brother Monmouth.

Despite King James's attempts to prevent them reading fiction, they were brought up on a diet of lurid romances. At the age of twelve, Mary began a correspondence with twenty-year-old Frances Apsley, whom Mary referred to as her 'dear husband'. Both girls adopted pet names – Clorine and Aurelia.

Clorine (Mary) wrote to 'dear dear dear dear dear dear' Aurelia (Frances): 'I may, if I can tell you how much I love you but I hope that is not doubted. I have given you proofs enough. If not, I will die to satisfy you, dear, dear, husband. If all all my hairs were lives, I would lose them all twenty times over to serve or satisfy you ... I love you with a flame more lasting than the vestals' fire. Thou art my life, my soul, my all that Heaven can give. Death's life with you, without you dear to love. What more can I say to persuade you that I love you with more zeal than any lover can. I love you with a love that never was known by man. I have for you excess of friendship more of love than any woman can for woman, and more love than ever the constantest lover had for his mistress. You are loved more than can be expressed by your ever obedient wife, very affectionate friend, humble servant, to kiss the ground where you go, to be your dog on a string, your fish in a net, your bird in a cage, your humble trout . . . '

Anne maintained a similar correspondence with Cecily Cornwallis, and then started exchanging letters with her sister's 'husband'. Anne and Frances were 'Ziphare' and 'Semandra'. But the former soon tired of Frances and transferred her affections to Sarah Jennings, six years her senior, leaving Mary in sole possession of Frances.

At fifteen, Mary was married off to William. It was not love at first sight. Although William was twenty seven, he was five inches shorter than his bride. Also, while she was attractive and healthy, he was spindly and sallow. When Mary was told that they were to be wed, she 'wept all afternoon and all the following day'. During the ceremony she could barely contain her sobbing, as she stood stiff and impassive. At the public bedding at St James's Palace, Charles II remarked with typical gusto: 'Now nephew, to your work! Hey! St. George for England!'.

Mary was heartbroken at the prospect of leaving England and her dear 'Aurelia', but it did not take her long to adapt to the bright and orderly lifestyle that she found in Holland. The Dutch palaces were light and airy, compared with the general decay and squalor she had known at St James's. The Dutch ladies were welcoming. Her retinue included a number of the girls from Richmond and, as a full-time soldier, William was frequently absent.

None the less, Mary did perform all her wifely duties. When she eventually became pregnant, she wrote to her beloved Frances: 'I have played the whore a little; because the sea parts us, you may believe that it is a bastard.'

She later suffered a miscarriage, the first of several. But William would go on trying for an heir. 'He comes to my chamber about supper time upon this condition,' Mary told a friend, 'that I will not tire him with multiplicity of question, but rather strive to recreate him ...'

Although William was not a man with an over-heated libido, he eventually sought comfort elsewhere. His secret mistress was Elizabeth Villiers, one of Mary and Anne's girlhood playmates at Richmond. Her great uncle was Buckingham, James I's lover. Charles II's mistress, Lady Castlemaine, was a cousin.

She was no beauty, especially when compared with the buxom Mary, and she 'squinted like a dragon,' according to her friend Jonathan Swift. 'One cannot imagine her arousing desire,' another observer wrote.

Elizabeth travelled with Mary's entourage in 1677 and almost immediately attracted William's advances. To discourage these she threw herself at Captain Wauchop, a Scottish mercenary. But to little avail. By 1679, the affair was the talk of Paris.

Mary knew that 'in two or three years men are always weary of their wives and look to a mistress as soon as they can get them.' William was discreet. He told her that he was working late on despatches. Mary accepted the lame excuse and, for five years, 'kept her sorrow locked away in her heart'. Her only consolation was her passionate correspondence with Frances Apsley.

Eventually, however, her father James II came to hear of the affair. As Protestants, the Oranges were a political threat to him and any marital disharmony would strengthen his position on the English throne. His spies in Mary's household began to gossip about William's infidelity and the British ambassador formally brought it to her attention. Humiliated in public, Mary waited outside Elizabeth's apartments one night and, at two o'clock in the morning, caught her husband creeping quietly out.

A terrible row ensued. She accused him of adultery, while he protested: 'What has given you so much pain is merely an amusement, there is no crime in it.' And he accused her servants of plotting against him.

William unburdened himself to Bentinck, who was, for once, unsympathetic. To have a wife was one thing; to have a mistress quite another.

Mary then tried to remove her rival. She sent Elizabeth – who was still one of her ladies-in-waiting – to England with a letter for the King. This contained the request that James should detain her there. But Elizabeth opened the letter on the way and, instead, delivered it to her own father. He advised her to go directly back to Holland.

When she arrived at the palace, Mary refused to see her and Bentinck also told her to leave. But when William heard about this, Mary was forced to take Elizabeth back into her employ. He also discovered that one of James's spies, Mary's chaplain, was reporting back that 'none but pimps and bawds must expect tolerable usage' and dismissed him, along with the British ambassador.

Mary learned to tolerate Elizabeth, who accompanied William and herself to England, when they became King and Queen. She was settled in a house near Kensington Palace and, for services rendered, Mary gave her 90,000 acres of James II's former estates in Ireland.

William and Mary considered their new kingdom to be 'a devil of a country, so dirty and wicked'. Mary sought to raise moral standards at court by introducing needlework which, she believed, 'took off ladies from that idleness which not only wasted their time but exposed them to many temptations.' William simply withdrew to Hampton Court with his mistress, to remove himself from London's social scene, which gave him 'an early and general disgust'.

Later, when the King was away fighting in Ireland, James's supporters spread the rumour that Elizabeth was pregnant and that William and Mary's marriage was breaking up. William responded with an act of breathtaking hypocrisy. According to John Evelyn: 'The impudence of both sexes being now so great and universal, persons of all ranks keeping their courtesans so publicly, the King lately directed a letter to his Bishops, to order the clergy to preach out against that sin.'

Meanwhile, he continued his own affair with Elizabeth Villiers with even greater discretion. Ironically, the event which put an end to this relationship was the death of Mary in 1694. In a final letter to her husband, Mary begged him to dismiss his mistress. Overcome with grief and remorse, William did just that. He gave her lands worth £30,000 a year and married her off to the Earl of Orkney. Although she was already forty, the marriage was blessed with three children.

The King did not remarry, nor take another mistress. Instead, he found a new royal favourite, a notorious libertine named Arnold Joost Van Keppel. This former page boy, like James I's lover Robert Carr, came to the King's attention when he fell off his horse and broke his leg. Bentinck, jealous of the younger man, warned that the King's growing intimacy with him was giving rise to rumours that they were having a homosexual affair. 'It is a most extraordinary thing that one could have no esteem or friendship for a young man without its being criminal,' retorted William.

William died in 1702 when his horse stumbled over a mole-hill – leaving the supporters of the Catholic Stuart line to toast 'the little gentleman in the black velvet waistcoat'. Mary's sister Anne then became Queen of England.

Charles II had married Anne off to Prince George of Denmark – even though he had little time for the youth. 'I've tried him drunk and I've tried him sober, but there's nothing to him,' the old King said. But there must have been something to George. He made Anne pregnant at least seventeen times, although none of the children survived infancy.

Anne, meanwhile, moved her old sweetheart, Sarah Jennings, into her household as lady of the bedchamber. In correspondence, they now referred to each other as Mrs Morley and Mrs Freeman. Describing their relationship in the third person, Sarah wrote: 'Every moment of absence she counted a sort of tedious lifeless state. To see her was a constant joy, and to part with her for never so short a time a constant uneasiness, as the Princess's own frequent expressions were. This worked even to the jealousy of her lover. She used to say she desired to possess her wholly and could hardly bear that she should ever escape this confinement into any other company ...

'She had too great a sense of her favour not to submit to all such inconveniences to oblige one she saw loved her to excess ... But though there was this passionate love on the one side and, as I verily believe, the sincerest friendship on the other, yet their tempers were not more different than their principles and notions on many occasions appeared to be.'

Sarah, too, was married. Her husband John Churchill was a soldier. Returning from his campaigns, Sarah recorded, he used to 'pleasure her with his boots on'. When James II had threatened to arrest his daughter and her husband to prevent them from joining William of Orange, Sarah had helped Anne reach safety while Churchill had delivered Prince George to William's camp. In gratitude, Churchill was made Duke of Marlborough.

Once on the throne, Mary tried to prevent Anne bringing Sarah to court. In response, Anne declared that she would 'shut myself up and never see the world more, but live where I may be forgotten by human kind.' She also told Sarah that 'if I had any inclination to part with dear Mrs Freeman it would make me keep her in spite of their teeth.' Then, in a move that was guaranteed to alienate the affections of her sister, Anne took Frances Apsley, the new Lady Bathurst, into her household.

When Anne became Queen, Sarah became the power behind the throne. At the same time, her husband's military prowess brought Britain great victories on the Continent.

Sarah now introduced her daughters into the royal household. She also found a place, as a lowly woman of the bedchamber, for a cousin called Abigail Hill, of whom it was said that she was prone to 'give ... a loose to her passion.' Sarah soon discovered that she was being supplanted in the Queen's affections. When Abigail married and became Mrs Masham, Sarah only heard of it by gossip, while the Queen was actually present at the wedding ceremony.

'My cousin was an absolute favourite,' Sarah wrote. 'Mrs Masham came often to the Queen, when the Prince was asleep, and was generally two hours in private with her.'

Sarah complained that Abigail 'could make a Queen stand on her head if she chose'. But the new favourite could not prevail on her mistress to elevate her to the peerage. When pressed, the Queen responded that it would 'give great offence to have a peeress lie on the floor' and, hence, not sleep in the royal bedchamber.

Rumours about the affair soon spread and, in 1708, a scurrilous ballad aappeared:

> *When as Queen Anne of great renown*
> *Great Britain's sceptre swayed,*
> *Besides the Church, she dearly loved*
> *A dirty chamber maid*
>
> *O! Abigail that was her name,*
> *She stich'd and starch'd full well,*
> *But how she pierc'd this royal heart.*
> *No mortal man can tell.*
>
> *However, for sweet service done*
> *And causes of great weight*
> *Her royal mistress made her, Oh!*
> *A minister of State.*

Her secretary she was not
Because she could not write
But had the conduct and the care
Of some dark deeds at night.

Count Grammont, a Frenchman visiting London, was greatly amused by the scandal surrounding the Queen's lesbian activities. The English, who were so sophisticated in some respects, were 'yet so uncivilized as never to have heard of that refinement in love of early Greece,' he wrote.

Sarah warned the Queen: ' ... I remember you said at the same time of all things in this world, you valued most your reputation, which I confess surpris'd me very much, that your Majesty should so soon mention that word after having discover'd so great a passion for such a woman, for sure there can bee noe great reputation in a thing so strange and unaccountable, to say no more of it, nor can I think that having no inclination for any but of one's own sex is enough to maintain such a character as I wish may still be yours.'

But Anne refused to end the affair and Sarah was so put out that, when Prince George died and Anne was consumed with grief, she tactlessly referred to the Queen's dead husband as 'that dreary corpse'. There were also suggestions in the House of Commons that Abigail should be sacked from the royal household. But Anne resisted these and demanded instead that Sarah should resign her position as Lady of the Bedchamber.

When Sarah left court, discrepancies were found in her accounts of the privy purse. This was used as blackmail when Sarah announced her intention to publish her version of life at Anne's court, including extracts from many of the Queen's letters. The embezzlement was covered up and Sarah delayed the publication of her memoirs until 1742, twenty-eight years after the death of the Queen. Inevitably, they caused a sensation.

Sarah's position at court was taken by the redheaded Duchess of Somerset, who was implicated in a scandal when a young suitor, Charles Königsmark, murdered her first husband. Jonathan Swift immediately leapt to her defence:

> Their cunnings mark [Königsmark] thou for I have been told
> They assassin when young and poison when old
> O root out these carrots [redheads], O thou whose name
> Is backwards and forwards always the same [Anna]
> And keep close to thee always that name
> Which backwards and forwards is almost the same [Masham].

The last years of Anne's reign witnessed a battle between the political factions supporting Lady Somerset and those supporting Mrs Masham. The Queen was perhaps too easily swayed by her maidservants and it was said that England was ruled from the bedchamber by dictators in petticoats.

7

THE ERECTOR OF
HANOVER

The death of the childless Queen Anne presented the country with a constitutional problem. There was little support for the Catholic Stuarts, so the crown was offered to Anne's distant cousin – and one-time suitor – George, Elector of Hanover.

George first came to England in 1690 to woo Anne. The preliminaries went well, but George's mother objected to her son marrying a commoner. Instead, he was married off to his sixteen-year-old cousin Sophia Dorothea, daughter of the Duke of Celle. She had been born out of wedlock and her father, the elder brother of George's father had originally been engaged to the latter's wife. Unwilling to settle down, the Duke of Celle rejected his fiancée and vowed never to marry. However, in later life, he fell in love with a French noblewoman who refused to be just a casual mistress. So they entered into a formal marriage arrangement, witnessed by the church. Some time after Sophia Dorothea's birth, however, they decided to have a more conventional wedding to legitimize the child.

This was normal practice in Hanover. George I's father, the Elector Ernest August, had many mistresses, including two sisters, Maria and Clara von Meisenbuch. He even shared Maria with his son for a brief period. Clara and her husband, Count von Platen, effectively ruled Hanover and milked the exchequer. Clara also bore Ernest's children and their daughter, Baroness von Kielmansegge, was to become George's mistress. He also bedded Clara's daughter-in-law, when she inherited the title of Countess von Platen. While George was entertaining himself in this incestuous fashion, his wife Sophia Dorothea decided that she, too, was due a little extra-marital fun. Her new partner was handsome Swedish soldier, Count Philip von Königsmark.

It was a passionate affair. After one bout of lovemaking, Königsmark wrote to Sophia: 'I slept like a king, and I hope you did the same. What joy, what pleasure, what enchantment have I not felt in your arms. God! What a night I have spent.'

'I would give half my blood to hold you in my arms,' was Sophia's devoted response.

Königsmark's superior officers were concerned about the relationship and questioned him. He replied that there was 'nothing in it', but when George was away on a military campaign, the couple grew less and less discreet, giving rise to rumours that they were about to elope.

Naturally, George was enraged by this – and so was Königsmark's former mistress, the Countess von Platen. It seems probable that she forged a note to the Swede in Sophia Dorothea's handwriting, beckoning him to her bedchamber. He was never seen again.

Inevitably, there were suspicions that he had been murdered and buried under the floor of his mistress's bedroom, or else that he had been dumped in the Liene River, in a sack weighted down with stones.

The affair hurt George deeply. In her letters to Königsmark, Sophia Dorothea had made disparaging remarks about his performance in bed. Shortly afterwards, they divorced on the grounds of her intention to desert him – a charge of adultery would have put the succession in jeopardy – and Sophia was incarcerated in Ahlden Castle until her death thirty-one years later.

If George had been involved in the murder, he displayed no signs of remorse, but continued to exhibit 'a healthy appetite for women'. He seemed to prefer women who were 'fat and complacent', which was seen as a tribute to 'the King's bad taste and strong stomach'.

When George I came to England, he left behind Countess von Platen, the only one of his mistresses who was remotely attractive. As a Catholic, she was deemed to be an unsuitable companion.

Instead, George brought with him two other mistresses, Ehrengard Melusine von Schulenburg and the Baroness von Kielmannsegg.

The former was described by George's mother, the Electress Sophia, as a scarecrow. 'You would scarcely believe that she had captivated my son,' she complained to a friend.

None the less, Ehrengard bore him three children – whose paternity he did not acknowledge – acted as a hostess at official functions and generally behaved as a wife. She was 'in effect, as much Queen of England as any woman was,' wrote Horace Walpole. They may even have entered into a morganatic marriage.

The Baroness von Kielmannsegg was George's half-sister. She was so 'corpulent and ample', wrote Walpole, that 'the mob of London were highly diverted at the importation of so uncommon a seraglio.' As a child, the diarist recalled 'being terrified of her enormous figure, the fierce black eyes, large and rolling between two lofty arched eyebrows, two acres of cheeks spread with crimson, an ocean of neck that overflowed and was not distinguished from the lower parts of her body, and no part of it restrained by stays.'

The Princess of Wales, drawing attention to the luxuriance of Kielmannsegg's make-up, remarked: 'She looks young, if one may judge by her complexion, not more than eighteen or twenty.'

'Aye, madam,' said Lord Chesterfield, 'eighteen or twenty stone.'

The British people were highly amused at this strange combination. Schulenburg and Kielmannsegg were described as 'the hop-pole and the elephant' or 'the may-pole and the Elephant and Castle'.

Lord Chesterfield remarked: 'The standard of His Majesty's tastes as exemplified in his mistresses makes all ladies who aspire to his favour, and who are near a suitable age, strain and swell themselves, like frogs in a fable, to rival the bulk and dignity of the ox. Some succeed, others burst.'

Despite this, women still flocked to the court in droves. On spotting Charles II's mistress, Louise de Keroualle, the Duchess of Portsmouth, and William III's mistress Elizabeth Villiers, Countess of Orkney, in King George's drawing room, James II's mistress Catherine

Sedley exclaimed: 'Who would have thought that we three whores should have met here?'

Schulenberg and Kielmannsegg both took bribes and made a fortune speculating on the South Sea Bubble and later used their influence to cover up their part in this financial scandal. Schulenberg, it was said, 'would have sold the King's honour for a shilling advance to the best bidder.'

One day, when her carriage was surrounded by an angry mob, she cried out in her imperfect English: 'Good pipple, what for you abuse us? We hef come for your own goodz.'

'And for our chattels, too,' came the reply.

George I never bothered to learn English. He lived in St James's or Kensington Palace, attended by his Turkish servants, Mahomet and Mustapha. He would spend his afternoons with Schulenberg and his evenings with Kielmannsegg.

His only attempts at getting to know his subjects better came from his efforts to seduce some of them. He turned his attention to the Duchess of Shrewsbury (an Italian by birth), the Duchess of Bolton, Lady Montagu (who was a noted expert on the harems of the Ottoman Empire), and Lady Cowper. They also accepted bribes from people who sought favours from the King.

When Lady Montagu arrived at court one day wearing a fine new pair of earrings, the Duchess of Marlborough remarked sourly: 'What an impudent creature to come with her bribe in her ear.'

Lady Montagu replied calmly: 'Madam, how should people know where wine is sold unless a sign is hung out?'

George I's advances to Lord Hervey's young wife caused much gossip and he also had a prolonged dalliance with the Countess of Macclesfield's young daughter, Anne Brett. As the latter had dark hair and skin, everyone assumed she was Spanish and called her 'the Sultana'.

'Miss Brett had an apartment given her in St James's Palace and was to have been created a countess,' recorded Walpole.

George made little secret of the fact that he had really only come to England for British gold and he spent as much time in Hanover as possible. He was on his way home for one of these visits when he died in 1727. By this time, the Baroness von Kielmannsegg and Sophia Dorothea were already dead – George had shown the fine delicacy of feeling for which he was renowned by going to the very theatre on the very night that he heard of his wife's death.

But Schulenburg survived him and seems to have been distraught at the news of his demise. Afterwards she kept a raven, which she firmly believed to be a reincarnation of the King, tending it lovingly for the rest of her life.

8

THE GORGEOUS GEORGES

Throughout his life, George II was deeply in love with his wife, Caroline of Anspach. She was a handsome woman and his appetite for her magnificent bosom never palled.

Nothing affected his devotion. When Caroline died he declared: 'I never saw a woman worthy to buckle her shoe.'

This did not mean, however, that he was always faithful to her. On the contrary, he took a great many mistresses, among them some of her ladies-in-waiting who did, indeed, buckle Caroline's shoe.

Even after the briefest separation, the royal couple would celebrate their reunion by rushing off to their private apartments. When together, they would spend every afternoon making love. George even had to be dragged from one of these bouts of passion when he was informed of the King's death and his own accession.

But no matter how much he loved his wife, George felt that it was his royal duty to take mistresses. As the

Vice-Chamberlain of the Royal Household, Lord Hervey, once remarked: 'Though he is incapable of being attached to any woman but his wife, he seemed to look upon his mistresses as a necessary appurtenance to his grandeur as a Prince rather than an addition to his pleasure.'

The political consequences of this were clear to Sir Robert Walpole. To gain political influence over the King, one had to curry favour with the Queen, rather than with his mistresses.

George's passions, according to Walpole, were Germany, the army and women. 'Both the latter had a mixture of the parade about them.' In marrying Caroline, he boasted that he had taken 'the right sow by the ear'.

His first mistress was Mary Bellenden, one of Caroline's ladies-in-waiting. The composer John Gay described her as: 'Smiling Mary, soft and fair as down.'

Mary found the affair both passionless and unrewarding. 'Though incontestably the most agreeable, the most insinuating and the most likeable woman of her time, made up of every ingredient likely to attach a lover,' wrote Lord Hervey, 'she began to find out that her situation was only the scandal of being the Prince's mistress without the pleasure, the confinement without the profit.'

This situation was made even worse by the crudeness of George's advances. One evening, while ogling her publicly at a royal ball, George began counting out the gold in his purse, as if he was about to buy her services.

'Sir, I can bear it no longer,' she said eventually. 'If you count your money once more I shall leave.'

He did. So she kicked over the pile of coins and stormed out of the room. Soon afterwards, she married the future Duke of Argyll. She then abandoned the court completely to go and live in the country.

Another notable beauty soon came to George's attention. Lord Chesterfield wrote of her:

> *Were I king of Great Britain*
> *To Choose a minister well*
> *And support the throne I sat on*
> *I'd have under me Molly Lepell.*
>
> *Heaven keep our good king from rising*
> *But that rising who's fitter to quell*
> *Than some lady with beauty surprising*
> *And who should that be by Lepell?*

But George II had inherited his true taste in women from his father. His next mistress was the plump and dowdy Henrietta Howard. She and her husband Charles were so poor that Henrietta was forced to sell her luxuriant trusses to a wigmaker in order to come to court. There, she took up a lowly position as woman of the bedchamber in Queen Caroline's household.

Although Henrietta had married for love, she found that her husband was 'wrong-headed, ill-tempered, obstinate, drunken, extravagant and brutal'. But she was ambitious and became George's mistress in return for a pension of £2,000 a year and the title of Lady Suffolk – a trifle compared to the usual expenses of royal mistresses.

The King used to go to her apartment every night at exactly seven – 'frequently walking up and down the gallery of an evening, looking at his watch for a quarter of an hour before seven, but would not go in until the hour struck'.

He would usually stay for several hours at a time. When a naive courtier suggested that they might be spending the time in conversation, Horace Walpole replied that she was so deaf and his 'passions were so indelicate' that they could not rise to such platonic pastimes.

Although Queen Caroline tolerated the affair, 'they hated one another very civilly'. Caroline took great delight in humiliating her woman of the bedchamber, forcing her to do the most menial tasks until her eyes were fierce with anger and 'her cheeks as red as your coat'.

The King did nothing to ease the situation. Once, when Henrietta had just finished tying a scarf around Caroline's neck, George immediately pulled it off again. 'Because you have an ugly neck yourself you love to hide the Queen's,' he scolded.

Henrietta's husband – who had risen to the position of Groom of the Bedchamber as a reward for his wife's amorous exertions – was little better. Overcome with jealousy, he ordered his wife to return to her conjugal duties and obtained a writ from the Lord Chief Justice authorizing him to seize her. Only the prospect of a £12,000 pension calmed him down.

However, Henrietta herself was well liked – 'civil to everybody, friendly to many, and unjust to none.' She refused to take bribes and won the respect of both Alexander Pope and Jonathan Swift.

She remained the royal mistress for twenty years. Then, at last, the King grew tired of her. Lord Hervey wrote: 'One would have imagined that the King, instead of dropping a mistress to give himself up entirely to his wife, had repudiated some virtuous, obedient and dutiful wife in order to abandon himself to the dissolute commerce and dangerous sway of some new favourite.'

The Queen immediately saw the danger and begged George to keep Henrietta. 'What the devil do you mean by trying to make an old, dull, deaf, peevish beast stay and plague me?' he retorted.

Henrietta, by now a widow, had the last laugh. She married again – this time to a man twelve years her junior.

George embarked on affairs with numerous young women; some, it was said, sent to him by the Queen. She knew that he would return to her and that he had always been frank and unrepentant about his physical needs.

He also spent a great deal of his time in his daughters' apartments, where he flirted with their governess, the young and wanton Lady Deloraine. She was married to the Duke of Monmouth's son, Mr Wyndham, who was a tutor to the King's son.

Lord Hervey feigned shock at this. 'Such is the lady who at present engages the dalliance of the King's looser hours, his Majesty having chosen not from any violence of passion but as a decent, convenient, natural and unexceptionable commerce, to make the governess of his two youngest daughters his whore and the guardian-director of his son's youth and morals his cuckold.'

Walpole was even more worried that this woman with 'a weak head, a pretty face, a lying tongue and a false heart' should gain influence over George.

'If she got the ear of anyone in power,' said Hervey cynically, 'it might be of a bad consequence, but since 'tis only the King, I think it is of no significance.'

Walpole consulted the Queen, who suggested that Lady Tankerville might be a 'safer fool'. She was a handsome, good-natured, simple woman 'to whom the King had formerly been coquet.'

'Send for Lady Tankerville,' Walpole reportedly cried, 'and place her every evening at commerce or quadrille in the King's way.'

Meanwhile, Walpole quizzed Lady Deloraine about the child she was carrying: 'That's a pretty boy, Lady Deloraine, who got it?'

'Mr Wyndham, upon my honour,' she replied immediately, 'but I will not promise whose the next one shall be.'

To the other ladies of the court, Lady Deloraine was adamant that she had never slept with the King, even though he had told her how unkind she was to refuse him and that 'he was sure my husband would not take it ill'. This appeared to mollify Lord Hervey who conceded that the King had to 'have some woman for the world to believe that he lay with her'.

Walpole thought that 'if she did consent she would be well paid,' especially as she had a younger man at home. But he soon concluded that she was no political threat – 'as she goes to bed with the King, lying with him or to him is much the same as lying to or with Mr Wyndham.'

Like his father, the King used to go back to Hanover every two years. Usually he spent his time there with Madame d'Elitz, a divorcée who 'had been catched in bed with a man twenty years ago and been divorced from her husband upon it'. Although she was no longer in the first flush of youth, Madame d'Elitz was nevertheless 'a handsome lady, with a great deal of wit, who had a thousand lovers,' among them his father, George I. 'There is nothing new under the son,' quipped one courtier, 'nor a grandson either.'

On one trip, George was introduced to Amelia Sophia von Walmoden, the niece of the younger Countess von Platen. She was twenty-one years his junior, married, with 'fine black eyes, and brown hair, and very well shaped'.

'It is not doubted that she will soon have an apartment at Kensington,' mused one observer.

The fifty-year-old King pursued her with unusual vigour and delicacy, and soon found her very accommodating. He sent back graphic accounts of the seduction to the Queen, assuring her that: 'I know you will love Madame Walmoden, because she loves me.'

Caroline was less understanding than George had expected. When he arrived back in London, suffering from a severe case of piles, he was in a foul temper and the couple immediately had a steaming row. This was partly due to his insistence on hanging a portrait of his new lover at the foot of their bed, and partly due to his tactless suggestion that Caroline should arrange a visit by the Princess of Modena as 'her Highness was pretty free of her person and he had the greatest inclination imaginable to pay his addresses to the daughter of the late Regent of France'.

However, this was a rare outburst. Normally, Caroline was much more amenable and the Archbishop of York praised her, saying that he 'was glad to find her Majesty so sensible a woman as to like her husband should divert himself'. For her own part, Caroline said 'she was sorry for the scandal it gave others, but for herself she minded it no more that his going to the close stool'.

The King's frequent trips to Hanover were, nevertheless, making him unpopular in Britain. Even Lord Hervey was angry that the British exchequer was being forced 'to support his Hanover bawdy-house in magnificence, and enrich his German pimps and whores'. In 1745, the Scots rebelled, although this rising was successfully put down by the King's brother, the Duke of Cumberland. But George still insisted on going back to see Madam von Walmoden the following spring, even though he was strongly advised against it. When checked, he became so irritable that 'everyone about him wished him gone almost as much as he himself wished to leave them'.

His absence did not escape public attention. A broken-down nag was let loose on the streets of London, with a sign around its head which announced: 'I am the King's Hanoverian Equipage going to fetch his Majesty and his whore to England.'

And someone pinned a note to the door of St James's Palace which read: 'Lost or strayed out of this house, a man who has left a wife and six children on the parish; whoever will give any tidings of him to the churchwardens of St James's Parish, so he may be got again, shall receive four shillings and sixpence. N.B. This reward will not be increased, nobody judging him to deserve a Crown.'

The Queen, anxious at the damage that was being done to the royal family wrote to George, urging him to hurry back with his mistress. Unconcerned, George replied to this with another long letter full of graphic details about his amorous activities. Henrietta Howard's old apartments were prepared, but the King returned alone.

By this time, the Queen was ill. She had tried to hide this from the King, who was terrified of disease. She was operated on without an anaesthetic. It was excruciatingly painful, but when the surgeon, who was probing her stomach with a knife, leaned over too far, bumped into a candle and set fire to his wife, she had to ask for a short break in the proceedings so that she could stop laughing. Queen Caroline's bowels burst. With typical gallows humour, Pope wrote:

> *Here lies, wrapped in forty thousand towels,*
> *The only proof that Caroline had bowels.*

On her deathbed, Queen Caroline begged her husband not to take another wife. As he wiped the tears from his eyes, he replied: 'No, I shall have mistresses.'

Lady Deloraine believed this was her opportunity. She had been coy before, but now she started bragging about her royal conquest, even to her wards, the King's young daughters. Walpole was resigned to the idea of the King having a 'plaything' but he wished 'His Majesty had taken someone less mischievous than that lying bitch'.

The death of the Queen created something of a political crisis. How were George's advisers to maintain their influence over the King? The Duke of Newcastle suggested that they should use his daughter, Princess Emily, as their intermediary.

'Does the Princess design to commit incest?' asked Walpole. 'Will she go to bed with the father? Does he desire that she should? If not, do not tell me the King intends to take a vow of chastity or that those that lie with him won't have the best interest in him.'

Walpole's solution was to send for Madame von Walmoden – on the grounds that he had been 'for the wife against the mistress' and now should be 'for the mistress against the daughter ... unless you think the daughter intends to behave so as to supply the place of both wife and mistress which ... I know not how she can do but by going to bed with him.'

In the meantime, George made do with Lady Deloraine. Even though he complained that she smelled of cheap Spanish wine, he slept with her 'without the least alteration in his manner of talking to her or his manner of paying her, and in short sent for this old acquaintance to his apartment for just the same motives that people send casually for a new one to a tavern'.

Lady Deloraine was discarded as soon as Madame von Walmoden arrived. The newcomer was created Lady Yarmouth and was installed as the King's official mistress. She was to prove a very effective power-broker. Lord Chesterfield remarked of the King: 'Even the wisest man, like a chameleon, takes without knowing it more or less the hue of what he is often upon.'

Lady Yarmouth also made money by selling honours, a trick that she had learned from the King. Shortly after her arrival in England, she had asked the King for £30,000. He refused but allowed her to choose two candidates for elevation to the peerage. She did so and, pocketing the bribes, she received the £30,000 without costing the King a single penny.

This was still a pittance when compared with the fortune accumulated by Madame de Pompadour, who was presiding at Versailles as Louis XV's mistress. A French count visiting London made a disparaging comparison between the pair. 'While Madame de Pompadour shares the absolute power of Louis XV,' he wrote, 'Lady Yarmouth shares the absolute impotence of George II.'

Like all Hanoverian kings, George II detested his son, describing Frederick, Prince of Wales as 'a monster and the greatest villain that was ever born'. Caroline shared this opinion, calling her son a rogue and claiming, without a shred of evidence, that he was impotent and had engaged another man to father his children. This was almost certainly a lie.

Frederick came to England when he was twenty-one, having already enjoyed the favours of Madame d'Elitz, who had been the mistress of both his father and his grandfather. Soon, he had 'had several mistresses and now keeps on, an apothecary's daughter of Kingston'.

'Like the rest of his race,' Walpole noted, 'beauty was not a necessary ingredient.' He was 'not nice in his choice,' it was said, 'and talks more of his feats this way than he acts.'

Frederick then turned his attention to Anne Vane, a 'fat and ill-shaped dwarf,' who was already the mistress of Lord Hervey and had, according to the Queen, 'lain with half the town'. Anne took up with Frederick while continuing the affair with Hervey, and deliberately caused a rift between the two friends to prevent them finding out. When she became pregnant, Frederick innocently claimed the child was his and set her up in a house in Soho Square. Hervey joined her in bed there and threatened to expose her infidelity unless she persuaded the Prince to take him back into favour.

Anne then confessed all to the Prince of Wales and the scandal became public. The merciless balladeers of the time dubbed her 'Vanella' and, when Frederick had a fling with her chambermaid, she left the court with Hervey.

Frederick later married seventeen-year-old Augusta of Saxe-Gotha, who was advised by Queen Caroline to be 'easy in regard to amours'. She bore him a son, George, while he took an older lover, Lady Archibald Hamilton, who had ten children.

In 1751, Frederick died suddenly, before coming to the throne. A contemporary epitaph ran:

> *Here lies poor Fred who was alive and is dead,*
> *Had it been his father I had much rather,*
> *Had it been his sister nobody would have missed her,*
> *Had it been his brother, still better than another,*
> *Had it been the whole generation, so much better for the*
>   *nation,*
> *But since it is Fred who was alive and is dead,*
> *There is no more to be said.*

Augusta brought up Frederick's son, the future George III, with the help of the puritanical Earl of Bute – the 'Presumptuous Prick,' as he was known – who was probably her lover.

When, eventually, George II died, he was buried next to Queen Caroline in St George's Chapel, Windsor. Their specially designed coffins had sides which could be raised, so that their bodies could come into contact once more.

The twenty-two-year-old George III then acceded to the throne. His puritanical upbringing led him to try to improve the image of the royal family, by ridding it of its reputation for sexual excess. However, his reforming zeal was hampered by his incipient madness.

The first evidence of George's moral stance came when Lady Yarmouth was sent packing back to Hanover with a strong-box that contained a £10,000 bequest left to her by George II. Sadly, for all his good intentions, George III was extremely susceptible to female beauty. Soon after his coronation, he fell passionately in love with the fifteen-year-old beauty, Lady Sarah Lennox, a great-granddaughter of Charles II, though he protested that he had never entertained 'any improper thought with regard to her'. He was also very taken with a Quaker, Hannah Lightfoot, though, eventually, his political duty forced him into a match with a German princess, Charlotte of Mecklenberg-Strelitz.

George was initially unenthusiastic about her, but after the wedding, he declared himself to be well satisfied with his wife's virtue and her unshakable sense of honour. Indeed, Charlotte was so dutiful that they eventually had fifteen children. In a mixture of gratitude and amazement, his contemporaries praised him for his 'resolute fidelity to a hideous Queen'.

While George III applied himself to this difficult moral task, the other members of the royal family showed rather less self-discipline. George's uncle, the Duke of Cumberland – the notorious 'Butcher of Culloden' – liked to indulge himself with actresses. There was a scandal when one of these was brought to Windsor by carriage, and then sent away on foot when she would not comply with his wishes. The King's brother, Prince Frederick, the Duke of York, was described as 'silly, frivolous and heartless, void alike of steadiness and principle; libertine in practice'. He married Mrs Clements, the illegitimate daughter of Walpole's brother. She was also the widow of George's childhood tutor – 'a depraved and utterly useless man'. The marriage collapsed in 1786.

Another brother, Prince Henry, Duke of Gloucester, flaunted his mistresses by driving them around Hyde Park in a coach bearing the royal coat of arms. His preference for married ladies led to Lord Grosvenor winning £10,000 in damages for the Prince's adultery with his wife. George III had only just paid out this fine when he learned that Henry had married his mistress, a young widow named Anne Horton, without his permission. Henry, the King declared, had the morals of a 'Newgate attorney' and he resolved to have 'no further intercourse with him'.

His sister, Princess Caroline Matilda, was married off at fifteen to King Christian VII of Denmark, a debauched and retarded homosexual. Johann Struensee consoled the young Queen and took over the government, but many of the nobility rebelled. Struensee was arrested and executed. Caroline was imprisoned and had to be rescued by a British fleet.

George III's determination to raise the standard of royal behaviour led to an important piece of legislation. In 1772, he introduced the Royal Marriage Act. This made the wedding of any of the royal children null and void unless it had received the express permission of the monarch.

This soon backfired, of course. The Act allowed George's sons to indulge themselves as much as they pleased, making engagements and even marriages, knowing that they had no force in law. In the House of

Commons, one minister suggested wryly that the title of the act should be amended to 'An Act for enlarging and Extending the Prerogative of the Crown, and for the Encouragement of Adultery and Fornication'.

George's royal children were kept in baby clothes long into their adolescence. Only three of his six daughters were ever allowed to marry. At thirty-one, Charlotte was wed to the Prince of Wurtemburg, who was so fat that Napoleon once quipped that the only reason for his existence was to see how far his skin could stretch without breaking. The other two royal brides married at forty and forty-eight respectively.

For all his strictures, George III had a great deal of trouble 'keeping under', as he put it, his own sexual nature. In 1789, as mental illness began to cloud his judgment, he declared himself to be passionately in love with Elizabeth, Countess of Pembroke – whom he called Queen Esther.

Elizabeth was a respectable middle-aged woman and was thoroughly embarrassed by the King's demented desires. George made long, rambling declarations of his undying passion and wrote graphic love letters to the Countess. It was a very delicate situation and finally the Archbishop of Canterbury intervened, warning the mortified dowager against taking any immoral advantage of the sick man's passions.

9

THE RANDY
REGENT

George III's attempts to stamp out the vices of the Hanoverian dynasty and to bring his son up to follow a strict moral code proved disastrous. The poet Leigh Hunt described George, the Prince Regent, as 'a violator of his word, a libertine head over heels in debt and disgrace, a despiser of domestic ties, the companion of gamblers and demi-reps' (women of doubtful reputation or suspected chastity). Hunt was fined £500 and sentenced to two years in jail for libel.

Following royal tradition, the Prince of Wales lost his virginity at sixteen to one of the Queen's maids of honour. Soon afterwards, his mother learned that he was keeping 'improper company' in his rooms after bedtime. His first new love was Mary Hamilton, the Duke of Hamilton's twenty-three-year-old daughter. When she rejected him, he fell for a much more amenable woman, Mary Robinson, an actress of dubious reputation. Born in Bristol, the daughter of an Irishman who had abandoned his family to set up a factory run by Eskimos on the Labrador coast, Mary was the wife of an articled clerk named Robinson. She gave birth to a daughter, but hard times followed and the couple were flung into jail for debt. On her release, Mary set about becoming a star of the London stage and improving her lot in life by whatever means necessary.

George first saw her playing Perdita in *A Winter's Tale*. Immediately besotted, he sent her locks of his hair and begged her to come to his apartments dressed as a boy. She resisted until, returning early from work one day, she caught her husband in bed with one of their maids. In revenge, she decided to sleep with George. Any pangs of conscience were quelled when the Prince promised to give her £21,000 on her twenty-first birthday.

They were often seen in public together, but the affair soon ended, leaving Mary with a sheaf of highly-charged letters addressed to 'Perdita' and signed 'Florizel'. She threatened to publish these and the King had to pay her off with £5,000 and a pension of £500 a year. He chastized his son angrily for getting into such a 'shameful scrape' at just seventeen.

Mary left for France where she became the mistress of the Duke of Orléans, returning eventually to settle down with Colonel Tarleton, the M.P. for Liverpool. In later life, she became paralyzed and George used to visit her regularly.

Despite the King's admonition, George continued with his dissipated lifestyle. He had a brief affair with Elizabeth Armistead, who later married the politician Charles Fox. Next, he had a fling with Mrs Grace Elliott, a wealthy divorcée. She claimed that her daughter was George's offspring and named her Georgina August

Frederica after him, although the father could just as easily have been either of the two other men she was entertaining at the time.

He might also have sired Lord Melbourne, the future Prime Minister, but his mother insisted that the father was Lord Egremont. George also had affairs with a well-rounded singer named Elizabeth Billington; August Campbell, the Duke of Argyll's daughter; the fox-hunting Countess of Salisbury, who was twelve years his senior; the great political hostess, the Duchess of Devonshire; and numerous other ladies of lesser fame, including actresses, singers, matrons, maids, courtiers and courtesans.

When he was eighteen he met the 'divinely pretty' Countess von Hardenburg, the wife of the Hanoverian ambassador. She caught his eye while playing cards and 'ye fatal tho' delightful passion arose in my bosom'.

'How I love her,' he declared. 'I would sacrifice everything to her. By heavens I shall go distracted. My brain shall split!'

George was so smitten that he 'dropped every other connexion of whatever sort or kind, and devoted myself entirely to this angelick little woman'.

The little woman in question was greatly impressed by this show of devotion but still kept her distance. Then George made himself ill and, out of pity, she gave herself to her young admirer. 'I enjoyed ye pleasures of Elyssium,' enthused George, after the event.

Count Karl August von Hardenburg learned about his wife's infidelity from the gossip column of the *Morning Herald* and wrote a stinging rebuke to the prince. His wife also wrote, saying that she hoped he had not forgotten all his vows and that she would willingly elope with him that very night.

In confusion and distress, George confessed everything to his mother. She 'cried excessively' and the youth simply fainted. It was left to the King to take the practical measure of expelling the von Hardenburgs. Not surprising, the Count soon left his post in the diplomatic service. Instead he went to work in Prussia, where he played an important role in Napoleon's wars.

The King wrote a long homily on 'your follies', in an attempt to save his son from further shame. It did no good. George fell into the company of Charles Fox, the radical politician and leading opponent of the King's ministers.

In his quest for the good life, the Prince became something of a playboy. He ate and drank too much and began to swell up. There were drunken brawls in both Vauxhall and Ranelagh Gardens. In 1789, at a thanksgiving service in St Paul's Cathedral, George and the other Princes were seen eating biscuits, chatting noisily and behaving most disrespectfully. The King complained that every day it was 'almost certain that some unpleasant mention of him could be found' in the newspapers.

The Times, for example, condemned the heir to the throne as a man 'who at all times would prefer a girl and a bottle to politics and a sermon'. The Duke of Wellington described him as 'the damndest millstone about the necks of any Government that can be imagined'. But George had a kinder opinion of himself, admitting that he was 'rather fond of wine and women'.

When George did settle down, he became even more of a problem. In 1784, he met Maria Fitzherbert. She was handsome, rich and six years his senior. He fell in love with her instantly and tried to stab himself when she refused his advances. A pious woman, Maria was genuinely frightened by his persistent demands that she should become his mistress and fled abroad.

The Prince of Wales 'cried by the hour, rolling on the floor, striking his forehead, tearing his hair, falling into hysterics, and swearing that he would abandon the country, forego the Crown, sell his jewels and plate, and scrape together a competence to fly with the object of his affections to America.' Faced with these antics, Maria stood firm. She would return only when he promised to marry her.

Legally, of course, this was impossible. George knew that he could not ask his father's consent, as required by the new Royal Marriage Act. Mrs Fitzherbert was twice divorced. Worse, she was a Catholic – and it was strictly forbidden for the heir to the throne to marry a Catholic under the 1701 Act of Settlement.

So George paid £500 to get an Anglican clergyman out of debtors' prison and, on the promise of a bishopric, he conducted a meaningless service and Maria was given a worthless marriage certificate. Later she admitted that she had 'given herself up to him, exacted no conditions, trusted to his honour, and set no value on the ceremony he insisted on having solemnized'.

They set up house together and soon George's marriage to 'Princess Fitz' was an open secret. He remained in love with her for the rest of his life and she bore him ten children.

But their relationship was far from easy. The Prince continued to gorge himself on food and drink, and grew steadily more violent. One night Maria had to hide behind the sofa while he searched for her with a drawn sword. He was also pathologically unfaithful. He had an illegitimate child by Lucy Howard and bedded Anna Crouch, the star of John Gay's *The Beggar's Opera*. Anna got £10,000 and some fine jewellery for what amounted to a few nights' work. In addition, George had to pay off her husband, a lieutenant in the Royal Navy, to prevent him from taking the matter to court. This cost him another £400. Then there was the matter of the passionate love letters he had so foolishly written.

Meanwhile, George had embarked on an affair with Lady Jersey, who had turned forty and was already a grandmother nine times over. She was known to have practised her formidable powers of seduction on both sexes.

After these exploits, the Prince was in debt to the tune of half a million pounds. Mrs Fitzherbert had to pawn her jewels to stave off the bailiffs. The situation left George with little alternative. He had to get married.

George III picked out a bride for his errant son, and the Prince of Wales agreed to go through with the ceremony, on the understanding that he would get an increased allowance. Unfortunately, the King made a disastrous choice. Caroline of Brunswick-Wolfenbuttel, the Prince of Wales's own cousin, was said to be 'exceedingly loose' even by German standards, 'where at that period they were not very nice about female delicacy'.

Lady Jersey was determined to sabotage the marriage from the outset. She delayed the royal coaches, so that there was no transport to collect Caroline on her arrival at Greenwich. Worse still, the royal couple loathed each other on sight. 'Pray get me a glass of brandy,' said the Prince of Wales. 'I am unwell.'

For her part, Caroline found the Prince 'very fat' and 'nothing as handsome as his portrait'.

Caroline herself was no beauty and her personal hygiene left much to he desired. The British envoy who was to conduct her to the Prince had first to persuade her to wash herself and her underwear. Whatever charms she might have possessed were hidden behind layers of make-up and unflattering gowns – the work, no doubt, of scheming Lady Jersey, who had inveigled herself into the position of Lady of the Bedchamber.

On the way to his wedding, George declared: 'I shall never love anyone but Mrs Fitzherbert.' He turned up late, drunk, and amused himself during the ceremony by ogling Lady Jersey. He then spent his wedding night asleep on the floor in a drunken stupor with his head resting in the fireplace. Amazingly, despite this highly inauspicious beginning, the Queen gave birth to a daughter, Charlotte, almost exactly nine months later.

Caroline of Brunswick soon realized that the Countess of Jersey, her own lady-in-waiting, was her husband's mistress. Bitter and humiliated, she confronted George and insisted that the Countess of Jersey should be sacked. But George considered that, with the birth of their daughter, he had done his duty regarding the succession and he told her bluntly that he had no intention of ever sleeping with her again.

Inevitably, the couple separated. The King was mortified and wrote to his son: 'You seem to look on your union with the Princess as merely of a private nature and totally put out of sight that as Heir Apparent of the

Crown your marriage is a public act, wherein the kingdom is concerned.'

George also turned his back on 'that Jezebel' Lady Jersey. He desperately wanted his 'real and true wife' back – Mrs Fitzherbert. He even amended his will, bequeathing a fortune in property to Mrs Fitzherbert while, 'to her who is called the Princess of Wales, I leave one shilling'.

It took four years to work his way back into Maria's affections. She even appealed to the Vatican for papal confirmation that renewed conjugal relations with George would be acceptable to the Church. The Pope assured her that, in the eyes of God, she was the true wife of the Prince of Wales.

George lost weight in a bid to impress her and spent freely on Carlton House and the Brighton Pavilion, even though the Napoleonic Wars were biting deep into the national purse. The Prince of Wales's only concession to the war effort was to drill a group of soldiers on Brighton Beach.

George's reconciliation with Mrs Fitzherbert did nothing to stop his womanizing. The Prince accepted the paternity of William Francis, son of a Miss Davis, and admitted siring George Seymour Crowe with Mrs Crowe of Charles Street. Luckily, his liaison with Anne, the French wife of Lord Masserine, produced no offspring. He also had a brief fling with a dancer called Louise Hillisberg and used to pay regular nocturnal visits to the apartments of Madame de Meyer.

The middle-aged Mrs Fitzherbert was philosophical about the prince's peccadillos with younger women. However, she was much less sanguine about his attachment to Isabella Seymour, Lady Hertford, one of the sturdy grandmothers who seemed to be to his taste. Princess Lieven described her as 'a luxurious abundance of flesh'.

George wrote long, loving letters to the matron declaring: 'I really do feel quite like a young colt going to be turned out to grass, as gay as a lark and as light as a feather.' He added: 'Pray tell Lord Hertford (with all that is kindest from me) that I shall he quite content if you are only half as glad to see me as I shall be rejoiced to see you.'

Napoleon apparently laughed aloud when he heard about the affair.

Meanwhile, George was also making grotesque passes at the portly Lady Bessborough, who was an old flame from his younger days. Lady Bessborough later recalled how George 'threw himself on his knees, and clasping me around, kissed my neck before I was aware of what he was doing. I screamed with vexation and fright. He continued sometimes struggling with me, sometimes sobbing and crying ... he would break with Mrs F and Lady H. I should make my own terms.'

Lady Bessborough did not know whether to laugh or cry at the sight of 'that immense, grotesque figure flouncing half on the couch, half on the ground'.

When the old King finally went and George became Regent, he dismissed the loyal Mrs Fitzherbert in favour of Lady Hertford, coldly stating: 'Madam, you have no place.'

George boldly asked Lady Hertford to 'live with him publicly'. Her husband had proof, of course, 'that HRH had been too familiar with her', but he chose to do nothing, as Lady Hertford's influence with the prince had gained him the post of Lord Chamberlain and had bought their son a position in the royal household.

After the breakdown of the royal marriage, Caroline of Brunswick moved to Blackheath, where she flirted outrageously at dinner parties and was frequently 'closeted with young men', the sort of behaviour that was said to be open 'to very unfavourable interpretations'. She also scandalized the neighbourhood by her friendship with Lady Douglas, who had already been ostracized by society. She, it was rumoured, had been having an affair with her husband's former commanding officer, Sir Sidney Smith. Lady Douglas and the Princess may have been more than just close friends, for the former recorded in her diary that the Princess would come 'upstairs to my bedchamber, kiss me, take me in her arms and tell me I was beautiful ... and [give me] such high flown compliments that women never used to pay one another.'

Caroline also boasted to Lady Douglas 'that she got a bedfellow wherever she could; that nothing was more healthy', and she even claimed, on one occasion, to be pregnant. When the two ladies eventually fell out, Caroline sent Sir John Douglas obscene drawings of his wife making love to Sir Sidney Smith.

In 1806, a committee of enquiry was convened to look into Caroline's behaviour. The 'Delicate Investigation', as it was called, examined every sordid detail of the Queen's sex life, including her relationship with Captain Manby, a naval officer who paid her frequent visits at Blackheath.

The committee's findings were summed up in verse by a contemporary satirist:

THE RANDY REGENT

Most gracious Queen we thee implore
To go away and sin no more;
Or if that effort be too great,
To go away at any rate.

And so Caroline did. She went off on a Grand Tour, partying her way across Europe with 'a particularly low set of people'.

Lady Bessborough spotted her at a ball 'with an extremely red face and a girl's white dress, with the shoulders, back and neck quite low (disgustingly so) down to the middle of her stomach ... and a wreath of light pink roses in her hair. Suddenly she nodded and smiled at me, and not recollecting her I was convinced that she was mad, till William Bentinck punched me and said: "Do you not see the Princess of Wales nodding at you?"'

Caroline set up home in Como with Bartolomeo Pergami, a former quartermaster in the Italian army. When the virgin Princess Charlotte, who had been strictly brought up by her maiden aunts in Windsor, went to pay her a visit, Caroline tried to ruin the girl's reputation by locking her alone in a bedroom with Captain Hesse. He was said to be the illegitimate son of George's brother, the Duke of York, and was one of Caroline's own lovers. Charlotte was eventually married off to a penniless German princeling and died in childbirth.

When the old King died and George IV ascended to the throne, he made one final attempt to rid himself of his unwanted Queen. He offered Caroline £50,000 a year if she would promise never to return to England. At the same time, the government drew up the Bill of Pains and Penalties to dissolve the marriage on the grounds of Caroline's adulteries. These allegations were investigated in lascivious detail by the House of Lords. Many witnesses were called. They related how Pergami had been present when the Queen was at her toilet with her bosom completely bare. He had fondled her naked breasts in public and had caressed her thighs. They had also slept with their arms around each other on a coach journey. He had been seen in her bedroom; with clothes; without clothes; in his underwear; in just a shirt. He had been present when she had taken a bath. They had slept together in a tent. The accusations seemed endless.

Caroline turned up to listen to the proceedings, while Pergami had the good sense to remain in Italy. But gradually, instead of condemning her, the Crown made itself look ridiculous. The King, after all, had been a lifelong lecher and what was sauce for the gander was sauce for the goose.

A London mob stopped the Duke of Wellington in the street and demanded that he shout: 'God Save the Queen.' 'Well, gentlemen, since you will have it so,' he replied, 'God Save the Queen – and may all your wives be like her.'

The government eventually had to drop the bill, but George was already planning his revenge. A resolution was passed that Caroline should not be crowned alongside the King in Westminster Abbey and, when she turned up to the coronation, she found herself unceremoniously excluded because she did not have a ticket.

When rumour came of Napoleon's death, the King was told his greatest enemy was dead. He replied: 'Is she, by God?'

Caroline eventually died in 1818. In celebration, George took himself a new mistress, the ample Lady Conyngham. She was married to a respectable Irish peer and had five grown-up children.

A scandal-sheet immortalized the meeting of these two generously proportioned physiques:

> *Tis pleasant at Seasons to see how they sit,*
> *First cracking their nuts, and then cracking their wit:*
> *Then quaffing their claret – then mingling their lips,*
> *Or tickling the fat about each other's hips.*
> *Give the devil his due, she's a prime bit of stuff,*
> *And for the flesh she's got conscience enough*
> *He'll never need pillows to keep his head,*
> *Whilst old Q and himself sleep and snore in one bed.*

This bizarre relationship seemed to give the King a new lease of life. Lady Cowper noted that George had said 'he never was so in love before in his life, that he's quite ashamed of being so boyish'. Meanwhile, the Foreign Secretary, George Canning, was ordered to dispatch Lady Conyngham's former lover, Lord Ponsonby, to Buenos Aires.

'I have never seen a man more in love,' wrote Princess Lieven, but, not surprisingly, Lady Hertford took a dimmer view of the affair. She found the King's 'new love ridiculous in view of the age of the contracting parties'. (Lady Conyngham and Lady Hertford were the same age.) Even so, she admitted that 'intimately as she had known the King, she had never ventured to speak to him on the subject of his mistresses'.

George's public behaviour did not improve with the passage of the years. In July 1821, while the Archbishop of York was delivering a sermon at Westminster Abbey on the sovereign's duty to protect his people 'from the contagion of vice and irreligion', the sovereign himself was seen 'nodding and winking, sighing and making eyes' at Lady Conyngham.

His influence with both government and the people was long since discredited. When Lady Hertford was pushed out of the royal bed and her husband resigned from his position as Lord Chamberlain, George did not even have the political clout to get the husband of his new lover, Lady Conyngham, appointed in his place. As Lord Holland later confessed: 'We all encouraged every species of satire against him and his mistresses.'

In his later years the dissolute King turned to opiates, in addition to his drinking. Doubtless, this was one of the reasons why George's obituary in *The Times*, published in 1830, displayed an unusual candour: 'There was never an individual less regretted of his fellow creatures.' Such was society's brutal verdict on its profligate monarch.

But perhaps the infamous Prince Regent did have one tiny spark of decency. His will gave instructions that he was to be buried with 'the picture of my beloved wife, my Maria Fitzherbert, suspended around my neck on a ribbon as I used to wear it when I lived, and placed right upon my heart.' When Mrs Fitzherbert heard of this posthumous tribute, 'some very large tears fell from her eyes'.

The four King Georges had ruled the country for over a century, from 1714 until 1830. None of them was greatly mourned, and the poet Walter Savage Landor wrote a stinging epitaph:

> *I sing the Georges four,*
> *For Providence could stand no more.*
> *Some say that far the worst*
> *of all was George the First.*
> *But yet by some 'tis reckoned*
> *That worse still was George the Second.*
> *And what mortal ever heard,*
> *Any good of George the Third?*
> *When George the Fourth from earth descended,*
> *Thank God the line of Georges ended.*

10

FOUR PLAY

As George IV had no legitimate children, the Crown had to pass to one of his brothers. The eldest of these was Frederick, the Duke of York, a man cast very much in the same mould as the King. In his private life he was dissolute and incompetent. As a soldier he was little better, and his inept leadership of the British expeditionary force to Flanders in 1793 was commemorated in the famous children's nursery rhyme:

The Grand Old Duke of York,
he had ten thousand men,
He marched them up to the top of the hill,
And he marched them down again.

During the period when the Prince of Wales was living with Mrs Fitzherbert, the Duke of York took it upon himself to make a more conventional marriage in order to secure the succession. Unfortunately, the bride he chose, Princes Frederica of Prussia, proved barren. So

Frederick began taking lovers, among them the notorious Letitia Smith, who was simultaneously sharing her favours with the highwayman John Rann.

When he was forty, the Duke of York settled down with Mary Anne Clarke, a bricklayer's daughter from Ball and Pin Alley, Chancery Lane, who was well known for her promiscuity. When the Duke abandoned Mary Anne Clarke for a Mrs Cary, she took up with Major Dillon and Colonel Wardle, MP for Salisbury. At her instigation, they both accused the Duke of taking bribes in order to secure the advancement of officers.

In the parliamentary enquiry, the Duke's love-letters were read out in public. Some were also reprinted in the newspapers. At the hearing, Mary Anne Clarke appeared in a daring silk dress and her answers to the ministers' questions were so saucy that one member passed her a note offering 300 guineas for the chance to have 'supper' with her.

Mary's allegations were supported by Elizabeth Taylor, a brothel-keeper from Chelsea. She reported a conversation in which the Duke had threatened to 'cut up' an officer who had insulted his mistress.

The scandal forced the Duke of York to resign his position as Commander-in-Chief of the armed forces. In addition, an effigy of him was mutilated by angry mobs in Yorkshire and Suffolk, protesting against the 'immorality of his life'. On a rather lighter level, when people tossed coins, they no longer called 'heads or tails', they said instead: 'Dukes or darlings'.

Mary went on to attack both Dillon and Wardle, claiming that they were in the pay of Frederick's younger brother, the Duke of Kent, who had offered her £10,000 to blacken the Prince's name. She later libelled the Chancellor of the Irish Exchequer and was sent to jail.

After this, the Duke of York was more cautious in his choice of mistresses, preferring aristocratic women, such as the Duchess of Rutland. He died three years before George and never succeeded to the throne.

William, Duke of Clarence, was the sailor of the family. He was sent away to sea at the tender age of thirteen after, it is said, seducing two of the Queen's maids of honour. Life in the navy gave him ample opportunity to practise what his elder brother called 'his natural inclination for all kinds of dissipation'.

On home leave when he was fifteen, he seduced his pretty young cousin Julia Fortescue. She was just fourteen years old. His parents quickly sent him back to sea.

There, he could satisfy his lust in the brothels of distant ports. He later said: 'The highest crime in Heaven next to murder is that of debauching innocent women.' The inference was that those who had already been debauched were fair game.

William was particularly fond of his voyages to the West Indies. On one of these, he caused damage to the value of £700 in a Mrs Pringle's high-class whorehouse in Bridgetown, Barbados. In Jamaica, he made a spirited speech in defence of slavery – because, it was said, he could practise both of his two principal passions, flogging and fornication, with the same unfortunate parties. He even brought back a West Indian concubine called 'Wowski' when he returned home.

William was sent to Hanover to complete his education. There, rumour had it, he entered into a secret marriage with Caroline von Lingsingen. Even if this was true, it did not prevent him making love, as he wrote to his brother, with 'women as poxied as whores . . . against a wall or in the middle of the parade-ground'. In view of this, it is remarkable that he only managed to contract veneral disease twice during this period.

'Oh for England and the pretty girls of Westminster,' he wrote, 'at least to such as would not clap or pox me every time I fucked.'

At nineteen, he fell in love with Sarah Martin – 'We dance and amuse ourselves greatly,' – until her father sent her away, fearing that the 'amusements' might have serious consequences. Next came Sally Winne, the daughter of a ship-chandler in Plymouth. Doubtless the Prince was glad to find some entertainment in the place, for on another occasion he condemned it, saying: 'Dullness rules here altogether, but what is worse than all, not a woman fit to be touched with tongs.' Finally, in Quebec, he managed to make the accommodating wife of the Surveyor-General pregnant.

George III was becoming tired of shuffling his wayward son around the colonies to avoid scandal. So he called him home, admonishing him for his 'love of low company ... immorality, vice, dissipation and expense.'

Certainly, family values meant little to William. On hearing of the break-up of the Prince of Wales's marriage, he said: 'My brother has behaved very foolishly. To be sure he married a very foolish, disagreeable person, but he should have made the best of a bad bargain, as my father has done.'

The Prince's enforced confinement in England made little difference to his behaviour. He bought a house in

Richmond and was soon cohabiting with Polly Finch, a well-known courtesan.

When he was twenty-five, William fell in love with an actress five years his senior, who went by the stage name of Mrs Jordan. Her real name was Dorothea Bland and she was the daughter of an Irish stage-hand. At twenty, she had given birth to a child by Richard Daly, a Dublin theatre manager. Then she came to London, where she became an overnight success after appearing in Garrick's *The Country Girl.*

She soon became the mistress of the theatre owner, Sir Richard Ford, and made her name in 'breeches parts' – her long, shapely legs made her an ideal choice for playing principal boy roles.

Dorothea was said to have 'fine animal spirits', but she also had a reputation for being vulgar and foul-mouthed – even by Regency standards. This was no problem for Prince William, who was often drunken and rowdy himself, and who also had a sizeable repertoire of salacious stories and jokes. Despite their obvious compatibility, however, he had to pursue the actress for eleven months before he could brag to his brothers: 'You may safely congratulate me on my success.'

The Times confirmed this in a more cryptic fashion: 'That the Jordan has crossed the Ford is a matter no longer to be doubted, and the Royal Admiral has hoisted his flag.'

The couple settled down and began a family. Over the next twenty years, they had ten children in all. It was hardly a conventional affair. As a bachelor prince, William had no money. So Mrs Jordan continued working to support their growing brood. The scandal sheets could not fail to be amused by the irony of the situation:

> *As Jordan's high and mighty squire*
> *Her playhouse profits deigns to skim*
> *Some folk audaciously enquire*
> *If he keeps her or she keeps him.*

William's parents appeared to give their tacit approval to the relationship. They even saw Dorothea perform on stage. And when a gunman loosed off a shot at George III, she led a rousing chorus of 'God Save the King'.

Even so, when she was fifty and had lost her figure, William abandoned her. This callous behaviour drew widespread public condemnation. One contemporary verse ran:

> *What, leave a woman to her tears?*
> *Your faithful friend for twenty years,*
> *One who gave up her youthful charms,*
> *The fond companion of your arms.*

Mrs Jordan was given a less than generous allowance and was told that she could keep her daughters, provided she did not return to the stage. She suddenly found herself landed with debts incurred by the son she had had by Richard Ford. She tried approaching William's brothers for help, but the royal family shunned her. So she was forced to give up her daughters and go back to acting. Then her health broke down and she had to flee abroad to escape her debts. Dorothea eventually died completely penniless and quite alone in France, a victim of her lover's ingratitude. Even her sheets had to be sold in order to pay for the funeral.

Prince William, meanwhile, had begun to stalk a rich heiress, to fund his extravagant lifestyle. She was Catherine Tylney-Long, who had an income of some £40,000 a year. She refused him, marrying instead a nephew of the Duke of Wellington, who promptly squandered her fortune.

Lady Charlotte Lindsay, Miss Mercer Elphinstone and the Dowager Lady Downshire also refused the Prince. The Countess of Berkeley, an attractive widow, was rather more willing, but she had been born plain Mary Cole, a butcher's daughter, and was the long-standing mistress of Lord Berkeley. The Prince was much too snobbish to put up with any such liaison.

So the rejections continued. William's cousin, Princess Sophia of Gloucester, also turned him down, and the Grand Duchess of Oldenburg described him as 'awkward, not without wit, but definitely unpleasant'.

The death of the Prince Regent's daughter Charlotte in 1817 made the matter even more urgent. But the Princess Royal of Denmark and two Princesses of Hesse soon joined the ever lengthening list of those who spurned the heir to the English throne. Meanwhile, William had fallen for the pretty, if vulgar, Miss Wyckham and she gladly accepted his proposal. On hearing the news, the Prince Regent groaned audibly and the government had to step in to halt the marriage.

Eventually, 'a poor wishy-washy thing', Princess Adelaide of Saxe-Coburg and Meiningen accepted the match. She was 'very ugly with a horrid complexion', but the Prince had no viable alternative. William did his best to sire an heir. Adelaide had five children, none of whom survived infancy.

Soon, the royal family were featuring in the scandal sheets again. There was gossip that Princess Adelaide had taken a lover – her Chamberlain Lord Howe. It was even rumoured that she was pregnant by him.

George IV's reign had been so unpopular that William feared for the future of the country. When he eventually came to the throne, at the age of sixty-five, he realized that the image of the royal family needed a radical overhaul. He tried to introduce a new moral tone by banning decolleté dresses at court, but the press were unimpressed. The *Morning Post* continued to complain about the indecent sight of the King riding around with Mrs Jordan's bastards in his carriage; Queen Adelaide also caused a scandal when she tried to meddle with the Reform Bill. And there were persistent rumours that William had fathered yet another illegitimate child by one of the Queen's maids of honour.

11

JOHN BROWN'S BODY

Although Queen Victoria is usually regarded as a paragon of virtue, some members of her family did not share her values. Her father Edward, Duke of Kent, for example, was vicious as well as corrupt.

After a number of youthful indiscretions, King George exiled him to Gibraltar. There, he commanded a regiment with a discipline that bordered on the sadistic. At the same time, to satisfy his lust, he sent an agent to France to find him a mistress. The latter returned with Julie St Laurent, a pretty woman whose origins are unknown.

Every morning, Prince Edward rose early to drill, inspect and, all too often, to flog his troops. They soon mutinied against this brutal regime, and Edward was posted to Montreal, where he continued his sadistic practices. On one occasion, he sentenced a scruffy soldier to 999 strokes of the lash. Not surprisingly, his men rebelled and Edward was posted back to the Rock.

There, he drew up a 300-page document, containing regulations for every aspect of garrison life, right down to the style of officers' haircuts. Soon, another crisis arose when he shut down the grog shops over Christmas. Whole regiments rebelled and Edward responded in his customary brutal fashion, hanging three and flogging dozens more. This time, he was sacked and recalled to England.

During these postings Edward had been accompanied by his mistress. When they set up home in England, he tried to give a veneer of respectability to his position by regularly attending church and patronizing worthy charities. Later, the couple had to flee to Brussels to escape their debts. The cost of living was cheaper there, but like his brothers, Edward was constantly in debt and the only way out of it was to marry.

The widowed Princess Victoria of Leinigen was deemed a desirable candidate, but Edward did not have the courage to explain the situation to his consort of twenty-five years standing. He even begged newspaper editors to keep it out of their columns. But eventually the *Morning Chronicle* published the announcement of the forthcoming royal wedding. One of the Continental papers picked it up and the unfortunate Julie finally learned the terrible truth at the breakfast table early one morning in 1816.

'It produced no heat or violence on her part,' noted Edward. Instead there was 'an extraordinary noise and a strong convulsive movement in Madame St Laurent's throat.'

Two months later, Prince Edward was married. Twenty-two months later he was dead. But during his brief marriage he managed to father Victoria.

The lifestyle of Edward's younger brother, Ernest, Duke of Cumberland, also attracted the scandal sheets. He was thought to have murdered his valet in a fit of rage. Rumour also had it that his wife, the twice-widowed Frederica of Mecklenburg-Strelitz, had lost her former husbands rather too conveniently. The inference was that she had helped them on their way. It was even alleged that Cumberland had plotted to poison Victoria, the only person who stood between him and the crown.

Prince Ernest was also believed to have carried on an incestuous relationship with his sister, Princess Sophia. They had committed all manner of sexual perversions, it was said, in the mirrored bedroom in St James's Palace. Gossip suggested that they might even have conceived a son.

Princess Sophia did indeed have an illegitimate child. Officially, the father was named as General Thomas Garth, an equerry at the Palace and thirty-three years Sophia's senior. However he was not dismissed, as one might have expected, and news of the whole affair was largely suppressed.

Further intrigues soon followed. Lady Lindhurst, the wife of the Lord Chancellor, accused Ernest of attempting to rape her in her own drawing-room, and Lord Graves slit his throat when he heard that the Prince was having an affair with his fifty-year-old wife.

A contemporary diarist wrote: 'There was never a man, of behaviour so atrocious as his – a mixture of narrow-mindedness, selfishness, trickery, duplicity, with no object but self, his own ease, and the gratification of his own fancies and prejudices.'

Cumberland's younger brother, Augustus Frederick was little better than his kinsmen. In Rome, in 1793, he fell in love with Lady Augusta Murray, who was several years his senior. Within days they had secretly married, in direct contravention of the Royal Marriage Act.

Returning to England, she became pregnant and they married again – this time openly in St George's, Hanover Square, under the names of Lady Murray and Mr Frederick Augustus. An ecclesiastical court ruled their marriage invalid. The King sent Augustus abroad and confiscated Lady Murray's passport to prevent her from joining him. Using forged papers, however, she managed to escape to Berlin with her son Augustus d'Este. There, they lived together for the next ten years. Eventually, Prince Augustus abandoned her, in return for an income of £12,000 a year and the Duchy of Sussex.

With the money in his pocket, Augustus successfully sued his former lover for custody of the children and deprived her of the title of Duchess. He then went on to contract another dubious marriage, this time to Lady Cecilia Buggin, the widow of a city grocer.

Although Queen Victoria could not actually acknowledge the match, she created Lady Buggin Duchess of Inverness. The couple attended formal functions as man and wife, but were bewilderingly introduced as 'His Royal Highness the Duke of Sussex and Her Grace the Duchess of Inverness'.

Only Adolphus, the Duke of Cambridge, managed to avoid the Hanoverian habit of attracting bad publicity. He livid in Germany with Augusta of Hesse-Cassel. However, the tendency towards mischief only lay dormant for a generation and soon reappeared with a vengeance in Adolphus's son, George Cambridge.

Shelley produced a damning summary of George III's recalcitrant sons:

> *An old, mad, despised and dying King;*
> *Princes, the dregs of their full race, who flow*
> *Through public scorn – mud from a muddy spring –*
> *Rulers who neither see nor feel nor know*
> *But leechlike to their fainting country cling*
> *Till they drop, blind in blood, without a blow.*

The behaviour of the royal princesses did nothing to redress the balance. Apart from the incestuous Sophia, there was Princess Augusta, who fell in love with Major-General Sir Brent Spencer, the King's equerry. She never dared ask her father whether she could marry him, but she did broach the subject with the Prince Regent, who forbade it. Even so, they may have married in secret or they may simply have remained lovers.

Princess Elizabeth set off rumours that she was pregnant, when she fell ill at the age of sixteen. Nothing came of this, however, and she had to wait until she was forty-seven before marrying the dull Prince of Hesse-Homburg.

Like Augusta, Princess Amelia fell for one of her father's equerries, a middle-aged Romeo named Sir Charles Fitzroy, who was descended from one of Charles II's bastards. No details of the affair are known, but the Princess considered herself to be his wife. When she died, she bequeathed her meagre possessions to her 'beloved Charles'.

Victoria herself was on very friendly terms with her uncle, King Leopold of the Belgians, the widower of the Prince Regent's daughter Charlotte. She probably knew of her father's long-term affair with Madame St Laurent. Even though it was never talked about at court, there were sometimes references to her father's 'old French lady' and the 'discovery of the St Lawrence'. But, as with the illegitimate children sired by her uncles, Victoria considered her father's murky past 'best forgotten'.

But Queen Victoria could not ignore her widowed mother's intimate relationship with Sir John Conroy, an Irish upstart. The Duke of Wellington certainly believed they were lovers and Victoria had witnessed 'some familiarities' between them. When she was young they tried to dominate her, aiming to rule the country themselves when Victoria became Queen.

However, Victoria found protection in her German governess, Louise Lehzen, and when she became Queen she gave orders for Conroy's exclusion from the court. But Sir John was not a man so easily thwarted and Victoria soon began to suspect that Lady Flora Hastings, one of her Ladies of the Bedchamber, was acting as a spy for Conroy.

After spending Christmas in Scotland in 1838, Lady Flora travelled back to London in a carriage shared with Conroy. Back at court, it was soon noticed that her belly was enlarged and that she was suffering from stomach pains. She refused to be examined by the royal physician Sir James Clark 'with her stays off'. Victoria quickly concluded that she was pregnant.

'We have no doubt that she is – to use plain words – with child!' she wrote in her diary. 'The horrid cause of all this is that Monster and Demon incarnate whose name I forebear to mention.' She meant, of course, Sir John Conroy.

When Lady Flora finally submitted to an examination, it was found that, while her womb was enlarged, she was still technically a virgin. It is not unknown for a woman to become pregnant without full intercourse taking place and with the hymen still intact. Privately, Victoria clung on to the belief that Flora had been guilty of misconduct with Conroy.

Although Lady Flora had been publicly cleared, the rumour still circulated that she was pregnant. The source of the gossip proved to be the Ladies of the Bedchamber. This coincided with a government crisis, in which Lord Melbourne lost office, and the new Prime Minister, Sir Robert Peel, demanded that the gossiping ladies should be dismissed. The young Queen refused. This caused a public outrage and mobs hurled abuse at Victoria, calling her 'Mrs Melbourne' – suggesting that the ex-Prime Minister had been more than just an adviser. Indeed, Melbourne, who had himself survived two scandalous divorces, once complimented the young Queen on her 'full and fine bust'. She was mortified at his downfall.

Commenting on the so-called 'Bedchamber Crisis' of 1839, the diarist Charles Greville wrote: 'It is a high trial of our institutions when the caprice of a girl of nineteen can overturn a great ministerial combination and when the most momentous matters of government and legislation are influenced by her pleasure about her Ladies of the Bedchamber.'

Victoria's treatment of Flora certainly made her very unpopular. At Ascot she was hissed at by the crowd. Eventually, she bowed to public pressure and, on 26th June 1839, went to see Lady Hastings, who was by then on her deathbed. She recorded in her diary: 'I found poor Lady Flora stretched on a couch looking as thin as anybody can be who is still alive, but the body very much swollen like a person who is with child.'

When Flora died on 5th July, it was found that she had a tumour on her liver. The *Morning Post* voiced the view of many when it accused the Queen of 'the most revolting virulence and indecency'.

Queen Victoria herself was not as strait-laced as is sometimes thought. She would often dance until three in the morning and declared that such 'dissipation' did her good.

When as a twenty-year-old Queen Victoria first met her cousin Prince Albert, she immediately fell deeply in love with him. After their second meeting, she commented: 'Albert's beauty is most striking.' At their third meeting, she asked him to marry her even though, she said, she was quite unworthy of him.

Brought up amid the depravity of the German court, Albert became a champion of moral rectitude. His mother, the Duchess of Saxe-Coburg-Gotha, had created a scandal by having an affair with the court's Jewish chamberlain – who may well have been Albert's real father. Then, when Albert was five, his parents divorced. His mother married an army officer and never saw her son again. Albert's father, Duke Ernst of Coburg, consoled himself with a series of mistresses and her name was never mentioned in his presence again. His brother was also a womanizer and paid for his carnal excesses by contracting syphilis.

Young Albert was sent to an all-male university and seems to have disliked physical contact with women. When he first heard of his cousin Victoria's interest in him, he wrote that he would not be 'corrupted' or 'brided' by her. Their wedding night must have been something of a disappointment for the amorous young Queen. 'Strange that the bridal night should be so short,' wrote Greville, 'and I told Lord Palmerston that this is not the way to provide us with a Prince of Wales'.

At Osborne House, Victoria decorated their bedroom with paintings of male nudes – perhaps hoping that it would stimulate her reluctant lover. Soon she was pregnant. In time, she had nine children by the prudish Albert.

The Prince laid down strict new rules for conduct in the royal household. Maids of honour had to meet gentlemen callers, even their own brothers, in a special waiting-room – never in the maids' private sitting-room. And no lady could be admitted to the royal drawing-room if there was the slightest stain on her reputation. A seventy-year-old woman who had run off in her youth with her schoolboy lover was refused admission – even though the couple had subsequently married and lived blameless lives together.

Similarly, Albert was outraged when the then Foreign Secretary, Lord Palmerston, forced his way into the bedroom of Mrs Brand, a lady of the bedchamber, and attempted to seduce her. The woman was unsporting enough to raise the alarm and a scandal ensued. Albert loftily considered that anyone capable of such a 'fiendish scheme' should be debarred from high office.

Queen Victoria, by contrast, firmly believed that a marriage was made in the bedroom and had, by all accounts, a robust sexual appetite. She hated being pregnant because Albert would abstain from sex for the entire gestation and the immediate post-natal period.

She would thus have to do without his affections for over a year.

She also loathed the act of giving birth: 'What you say of the pride of giving life to an immortal soul is very fine dear,' she wrote to her daughter Vicky, when she was about to have her first child, 'but I own I cannot enter into that; I think much more of our being like a cow or a dog at such moments; when our poor nature becomes so very animal and unecstatic'.

Unfortunately for her, Albert believed that sex was for procreation, not recreation. When she was told that her ninth child must be her last, she replied: 'Can I have no more fun in bed?'

After Albert's death, the Queen lamented: 'What a dreadful going to bed. What a contrast to that tender lover's love. All alone!' She went into extravagant and protracted mourning. None the less, she still surrounded herself with 'handsome and attractive girls for the maids of honour' and got grumpy and jealous when they left to marry.

Victoria also forged lasting friendships with several men who helped and advised her. One of these was John Brown, her chief gillie at Balmoral. Before Albert's death, he had cared for the Queen's ponies. Afterwards, they began to spend more time together. He dominated her in his gruff way, calling her 'woman' and chiding her if she was dressed too lightly for a brisk Scottish ride.

Within five years of Albert's death, John Brown's salary had increased five-fold and he had been given a cottage at Balmoral. This raised him to the status of 'Esquire' and placed him high in rank above the other servants. There were rumours that they had secretly married and the newspapers referred to her as 'Mrs Brown'.

Queen Victoria also fell under the thrall of the charming and flirtatious Benjamin Disraeli. In his youth he had been an incorrigible womanizer and his tastes had often run to older women – indeed, he had married one.

After the death of John Brown, Victoria's Indian servant, Abdul Karim, assumed a similar role in her life. He had come to England aged twenty-four at the time of her Golden Jubilee. She called him Munshi, appointed him as her secretary, and gave him a cottage at Windsor with a staff of his own. She also defended him against claims that he was a spy and would not listen to those who said that it was inappropriate for her to be intimate with a 'black man' a term she abhorred.

When Queen Victoria died, one of the first acts of the new King was to remove the statue of John Brown that stood in the hallway at Balmoral. It now stands in the woods nearby and is overgrown with ivy. Similarly, when Munshi died, the King had all his papers burned, perhaps to destroy anything incriminating.

12

EDWARD THE CARESSER

The Prince of Wales was a constant disappointment to his upright parents. In Albert Edward – or, more commonly, just plain Bertie – the Hanoverian taste for mischief reasserted itself strongly.

The first signs of his licentious nature were revealed when the fifteen-year-old Prince was sent to Königswinter on the Rhine to improve his German. He made a grab for a serving girl and tried to kiss her. Prime Minister William Gladstone, a strict Christian who dedicated himself to the reform of fallen women, described the incident as 'this squalid debauch, a paltry affair, an unworthy indulgence'.

At Oxford, despite the close attention of his chaperone, the Prince of Wales managed to spend much of his time with Sir Frederick Johnstone, a member of the notorious Bullingdon Club. And, oven though the dour martinet, General Bruce, had been appointed to watch his every move, the Prince embarked on a life of excess smoking, drinking and gluttony.

Oxford provided a rather different education to the one his parents had hoped for. There, Bertie gained an intimate knowledge of gambling, horses and the gilded life of the English aristocrat. One friend he particularly admired was the sophisticated, flamboyant and hugely rich Henry Chaplin, aptly nicknamed the 'Magnifico'. Chaplin had hired his own private chef to provide sumptuous gourmet feasts for himself and his companions. He would also saunter into chapel wearing an immaculately tailored hunting coat under the regulation surplice. One story of the time recounted how Bertie and the 'Magnifico', meeting an old peasant woman on a country road, pulled her skirt up over her head and stuck a five pound note in her bloomers.

All the Christchurch rips were dedicated womanizers. Listening to them boast about their adventures with actresses, married women and even grand society hostesses was enough to make any young man's blood race. Through them, the Prince of Wales learned of the wild times to be had in London – of the dogfights, the boxing matches, the opium dens and the brothels. It also brought home to him just how difficult it was for a royal prince to satisfy his natural urges.

In March 1861, when he was nineteen, the Prince of Wales joined the army and was sent to the Curragh military camp near Dublin. One night, after a particularly rowdy and drunken mess party, some fellow officers hid a naked young woman, an actress called Nellie Clifden, in his bed. The Prince of Wales was absolutely enchanted by the attractive girl and began an affair with her. This soon became common knowledge and Nellie basked in the glory of being nicknamed 'the Princess of Wales' by the London gossips.

Now aware of the Prince's nature, Victoria and Albert thought that his youthful lusts had better be contained within the sanctity of an early marriage and they began to search for a suitable bride for him. Of the seven suggestions named in *The Times*, a Danish Princess, Alexandra of Schleswig-Holstein-Sonderburg-Glucksburg, came fifth on the list. One major objection against her was that her mother was a princess of Hesse-Cassel, the most debauched court in Europe.

But Edward's sister Vicky favoured her, though she pitied anyone who had to marry the lecherous Bertie. 'I love him with all my heart and soul but I do not envy his future wife,' she wrote.

The Prince of Wales was equally enchanted by the delightful sixteen-year-old Princess and he told his parents that he 'thought her very charming and pretty', but he felt that he was not quite yet ready for marriage.

It was at this juncture that news of the Prince's escapade with Nellie Clifden reached the ears of the Queen. Lord Torrington, who was always in touch with the latest London gossip, confirmed the story. Worse still, Nellie had not even remained faithful to the Prince. She was now sharing her affections with Charles Wynn-Carrington.

Prince Albert was appalled. He wrote that his son must not be lost – 'the consequences for this country and for the world would be too dreadful.' But as he travelled up to Cambridge to scold his son, he caught typhoid fever and died.

The Queen blamed Bertie for his father's death. She later wrote: 'Oh, that boy. Much as I pity him, I never can, or shall, look at him without a shudder.'

Victoria now deemed marriage urgent. The Prince of Wales proposed to Princess Alexandra and was immediately accepted, even though the latter was under no illusions about the likely behaviour of her fiancé. 'If he were a cowboy, I should love him just the same and marry no one else.'

The wedding took place on 10th March 1863 in St George's Chapel, Windsor. There were about 900 guests, making it a small affair in comparison with the wedding of the current Prince of Wales and Lady Diana Spencer in 1981, when there were some 3,500 guests. However, Alix's father, Christian IX, was not invited; his reputation for promiscuity had made him too notorious for Victoria's liking.

With his marriage to Alexandra, the Prince of Wales freed himself from the immediate control of his mother and her sombre court. Repression, restraint and self-denial were now behind him and he could return to the way of life he enjoyed.

At the beginning of April, the newly-weds moved into Marlborough House, the Prince's private residence in Pall Mall. At last the master of his own home, Bertie could now let the royal jamboree begin in earnest. Soon his life was a mad whirl of banquets, balls, garden parties, evenings at the opera and gala celebrations, where the feasting and dancing went on until dawn. There were also long nights spent playing baccarat and wild men-only parties complete with bevies of chorus-girls.

Fashionable London rejoiced. Royalty hadn't been seen to enjoy itself so much for over thirty years, since the reign of gouty old George IV. The Prince of Wales immediately assumed leadership of the smart social scene. There was nothing now to prevent him from indulging his appetite for racy talk, rich food, hunting, gambling, good cigars and, of course, pretty women.

That he loved his wife, and was proud of the beauty, elegance and dignity which she brought to her role, was obvious. Equally clear, right from the start, was that while other less hampered young men sowed their wild oats before marriage, the Prince of Wales was sowing his afterwards. And when Alexandra fell pregnant and was required to spend more time at home resting, the Prince of Wales relished the opportunity to go gallivanting without her.

During that first wonderful year of his marriage, the Prince of Wales laid the pattern for the rest of his life: the pursuit of pleasure. And that pleasure was always to be found in the same places – the racetrack, the ballroom, the dinner table and the beds of beautiful women.

At Marlborough House and Sandringham he was a faultless host. As a husband he was notoriously unfaithful but not uncaring, and to his children he was a tolerant, affectionate and undemanding father. His friends adored him and constantly praised his kindness and loyalty – even those whose wives he slept with seemed to feel they'd been accorded a royal honour. The only person he failed to impress was his mother, the Queen.

She was kept fully informed about all his antics and wrote a steady stream of letters criticizing his life, his friends and the dreadful example he set for the rest of society. She was also horrified to learn that he had taken up the shocking habit of smoking.

In January 1864, the Prince and Princess of Wales were at Frogmore House when Prince Albert – known universally as 'Eddy' – was born, two months premature. Eighteen months later Prince George was born, again prematurely.

This time the confinement was at Alexandra's home in Denmark. But the Prince of Wales found the Danish court so dull that he excused himself and popped over to Stockholm, where King Charles XV of Sweden entertained him with some accommodating ladies. Queen Victoria knew the situation and felt sorry for Alexandra: 'I often think her lot is not an easy one, but she is fond of Bertie, though not blind.'

For those who had a hankering for such things, Victorian London was a tawdry den of vice. Young aristocrats would slum it in the sailors' dives in Rotherhithe, or in the squalid drinking taverns and brothels of Leicester Square. Then there were the infamous child brothels around Spitalfields. Elsewhere, hordes of cheap whores solicited for business up and down the Haymarket and the Waterloo Road. For those with more expensive tastes, there were the houses in Mayfair and Chelsea, where champagne flowed and carnal appetites could be indulged in an atmosphere of extravagance and luxury.

In 1860, it was estimated that there were 80,000 prostitutes in London alone. Some of them became famous, fêted beauties who were courted by gentlemen of wealth and position. These included Polly Ash, 'Sweet Nellie' Fowler – so-called because of her natural body scent – and Laura Bell, who became an evangelical preacher when she retired from her youthful calling. Queen of the courtesans was 'Skittles', who hailed from Liverpool.

The young Earl of Hartington – the future Duke of Devonshire – begged her to marry him, but she enjoyed her promiscuous ways too much. She had won her nickname, it was said, when she knocked down a group of drunken Guards officers 'like a row of skittles'.

When wealthy rakes and the young bloods of the nobility stepped out for a night on the town, their itinerary inevitably included the rounds of the fashionable London clubs. In these establishments they could drink, dance, flirt and behave outrageously without fear of censure. One of the most celebrated was Mott's Dancing Rooms in Foley Street, near Tottenham Court Road. This was run by the elegant and snobbish Mr Freer. He prided himself on the pedigree of his clientele – whose pranks he tolerated as long as they were sufficiently aristocratic. Another source of pride was the good looks and discretion of his 'ladies'.

Bigger, though less exclusive, was Cremorne Gardens in Chelsea. This had private boxes where gentlemen could wine, dine and recline with their mistresses, away from prying eyes. And for particularly amorous couples there was always the 'Hermit's Cave' and the 'Fairy Bower'.

The twenty-three-year-old Marquis of Hastings was one of those responsible for introducing the Prince of Wales to the capital's low life. He was good looking, outrageously rich and thoroughly irresponsible. Hastings was a regular at the illegal cock fights held at Faultless Pit in Endell Street, where he often matched his birds with those of the Duke of Hamilton. He also attended 'racing matches', where young aristocrats laid bets on how many rodents a terrier could kill in the space of an hour. As a practical joker he became famous when he released two hundred sewer rats on to the crowded dance-floor of a chic London club.

Photography was still in its infancy and Edward's face was therefore relatively unknown. So he was free to roam the city in search of fun with his roistering cronies in comparative privacy. This anonymity also allowed him to enjoy the very simple pleasures that others took for granted – like being driven around in an ordinary hansom cab and having a young wench in the back.

Generally, though, the Prince of Wales preferred to indulge himself abroad, in Egypt or in the fashionable spa towns of Germany. Every year after the Regatta at Cowes, he moved on to take the waters. He visited Homburg, Baden-Baden and then, in 1899, discovered Marienbad. Officially he went for his health and he usually managed to lose around eight pounds.

The real reason, however, was that the spas were teeming with grand society ladies, famous courtesans and regiments of women from the *demi-monde*. One of the many women to be honoured by his attentions was the proprietor of a hat shop, the delightfully pretty Fraulein Pistl. Another was Sophie Hall Walker, whose husband bred the Prince's Derby winner, 'Minoru'.

One prostitute travelled all the way from Vienna simply in order to sleep with him. When she found that the Prince of Wales was already amorously engaged, she demanded that one of the other gentlemen of his entourage partner her in order to cover her train fare.

But it was the brothels of Paris that were the Prince of Wales's true spiritual home. His favourite was Le Chabanais – the chair he sat in to make his selection of girls was still on display there a generation later. When the Duc de Gramont took him to La Maison Dorée to meet the famous prostitute Guilia Beneni – better known as La Barucci – she turned her back on the Prince and pulled up her skirts. She was naked underneath. When the Duc remonstrated, La Barucci – who once claimed to be the 'greatest whore in the world' – said candidly: 'You told me to show him my best side.'

Flamboyant excess had reached a glittering peak in the French capital during the 1860s. The aristocracy dedicated itself to all the diverse pleasures of the flesh and love was elevated to the status of an art form.

It was the golden age of the *grandes cocottes* – also known as *les horizonatales* – the pampered courtesans who were Paris's most glamorous celebrities. Through their skills in the bedroom, these women were able to amass huge fortunes and managed to maintain luxurious residences with retinues of liveried servants.

Among the most famous were La Pavia, who lived in a mansion on the Champs Elysées; Blanche d'Artigny, the model for Zola's Nana; Catherine Walters, an English girl; and Cora Pearl, who was from Plymouth and who was once paid £10,000 for a single night with Emperor Napoleon III. When the Prince of Wales asked to see Cora, she had herself served up at his dinner-table on a silver salver. When the cover was removed, she was completely naked except for a string of pearls and a sprig of parsley.

The actress and singer Hortense Schneider was another favourite of the Prince of Wales. She was so much in demand with foreign nobility that she earned herself the title of '*Le Passage des Princes*'.

The Times picked up the rumours from France and published a report about Edward's 'friendship' with Hortense. Little thinking that his exploits in Paris or the

Riviera would cross the Channel, the Prince had seen no reason to be careful when visiting her dressing-room, calling at her home or taking her out to dinner. For her part Hortense, like Nellie Clifden before her, was only too eager to boost her status by bragging about her royal beau.

From then on, the Prince of Wales was more discreet. He spoke excellent French and passed himself off as the Duke of Lancaster or the Earl of Chester. This fooled no one. When he visited the Moulin Rouge, the dancer La Goulue would shout out: 'Hello, Wales.' He would smile at this and then order champagne for the orchestra.

The Prince of Wales adored the *demi-monde* of Paris and was just as happy to sleep with a stylish harlot as with a titled lady. He first met Princesse de Sagan, the lovely and lascivious daughter of a banker, at the court of Empress Eugénie at Fontainebleau in 1867. Her husband was a hugely rich, stylish man, famous as both a wit and *raconteur*. Tough, amusing and sexy, de Sagan enticed Bertie to join her entourage of lovers. Once they had started the affair, she soon became his principal French mistress, maintaining her dominance well into the 1880s.

It was a curious love-hate relationship. Both continued to have legions of other lovers and enjoyed making repeated barbed remarks at the other's expense.

But the Princess relished her role as Edward's lover and always entertained him in the most sumptuous style. For his part, he adored the magnificent Sagan mansion in the Rue St Dominique and her enormous castle, south of Paris in Mello. Each spring, they spent time together at her beautiful estate in Cannes.

Although de Sagan's long-suffering husband bore her infidelity with the self-control demanded of his caste, her eldest son did not. Returning early one day to find a gentleman's clothes strewn around her boudoir, he picked them up and threw them into the fountain.

Edward emerged from the bedroom with nothing to wear and had to traipse back to his hotel in a pair of borrowed, too tight trousers. The offending youth was banished from the family home, although his outrage may have been well founded. The Prince of Wales was rumoured to be the father of de Sagan's youngest child.

Edward was not content to leave this kind of lifestyle behind in France. He imported his Parisian pastimes into England. When the Earl of Rosebery was asked to allow his London home to be used by the Prince for entertaining chorus-girls and other willing young women, he was shocked. However, Lord Carrington obliged and the Prince of Wales employed his house for his afternoon diversions, later changing the venue to Rosa Lewis's famous Cavendish Hotel in Jermyn Street.

The Prince of Wales's disreputable goings-on with chorus-girls, actresses and prostitutes hardly caused a stir. But his affair with a married woman, Harriet Mordaunt, turned into a huge scandal. She was an attractive woman of twenty-one, married to the rich, pigeon-shooting MP, Sir Charles Mordaunt, who had been a frequent guest at the Prince's parties at Marlborough House. Throughout 1867 and 1868, the Prince of Wales made a habit of visiting Harriet at home several times a week. He sent her discreet letters and even a Valentine card, but eventually the relationship petered out. Lord

Cole and Sir Frederick Johnstone, both friends of the Prince from his Oxford days, took over from him as her suitors.

Then in 1869 Harriet gave birth to her first child. The infant had a chronic eye condition. The young mother was beside herself with guilt and despair, and confessed all to her husband. Their baby's affliction, she told him, had been caused by her terrible wickedness. She had 'done very wrong with Lord Cole, Sir Frederick Johnstone, the Prince of Wales and others'.

In Victorian high society, many cuckolded husbands preferred to keep their skeletons locked firmly in the cupboard, but Sir Charles decided otherwise. Instead, he did the unforgivable. He took a compromising diary and the Prince of Wales's letters from his wife's locked writing desk and filed for divorce.

The scandal became public when Edward was summoned to appear in the divorce court. Both his wife, the long-suffering Alexandra, and, more surprisingly, Queen Victoria gave him their loyalty and full support.

The Lord Chancellor read the letters and declared them to be 'unexceptional in every way' and the judge assured the Prince that he would protect him from any 'improper questions'. But when the Prince of Wales appeared in the witness box, he was asked: 'Has there ever been any improper familiarity or criminal act between yourself and Lady Mordaunt?' He thought for a moment, then replied, firmly and decisively: 'No, never!'

With the strain of the trial, Harriet Mordaunt's mental condition deteriorated dramatically. She was declared insane and committed to a lunatic asylum. This prevented her from being a party to the suit and the case was dismissed.

After the trial, *Reynold's Newspaper* accused the Prince of Wales of being 'an accomplice to bringing dishonour to the homestead of an English gentleman'. A meeting in Hyde Park called for the abolition of the monarchy. Crowds booed him when he arrived at the Olympic Theatre with Alexandra, and again at Ascot.

Despite the growing public interest in his conduct, Edward took to consoling the recently widowed Lady Susan Pelham-Clinton. In 1871, she wrote to him commending him on his kindness over the last few years. But she was seven months pregnant at the time and lamented: 'Without any funds to meet the necessary expenses and to buy the discretion of servants, it is impossible to keep this sad secret.'

She was given £250 and packed off to Ramsgate, accompanied by the Prince of Wales's personal physician. This sort of pregnancy was obviously a slip-up, but there had been other children. One lived to a ripe old age in La Jolla, California. Plainly, the Prince of Wales was not the type of man to take precautions.

In the early nineteenth century, contraception was mainly a matter of caution and self-restraint combined with a large measure of luck. Couples usually relied on *coitus interruptus* – if they attempted any form of birth control at all.

But from about 1820, doctors began researching methods of contraception, often under the guise of 'Neo-Malthusianism'. In the eighteenth century, Thomas Malthus had predicted that there was going to be a massive population explosion which the world did not have the resources to sustain. Poverty and starvation, he argued, would be the inevitable result.

The Victorians were concerned by Malthus's predictions, as the rate of population growth was beginning to spiral out of control. This resulted not only from the high birth rate, but also from new medical discoveries and better sanitation. People were surviving childhood and living longer. However, after the 1870s the birth rate took a sudden dive.

A young Scottish doctor called George Drysdale had written the first book on birth control. It was called *Physical, Sexual and Natural Religion.* In the book, Drysdale gave detailed descriptions of such contraceptive techniques as withdrawal, the rhythm method, using a sponge or douching with tepid water, and the use of sheaths.

Withdrawal was plainly unsatisfactory and unreliable. Theories about the rhythm method – only having intercourse at certain times of the month – were just developing at this time, as medical research revealed new information about the circumstances under which conception took place.

As an alternative, Drysdale recommended the considerably less reliable sponge method because 'any preventative means, to be satisfactory, must be used by the woman, as it spoils the passion and impulsiveness of the venereal act if the man has to think of them ... ' This precluded the use of sheaths.

Condoms had been on sale in London since 1776, but they were unreliable, as well as expensive. They were made of linen, animal gut or fish skin and were difficult to use. However, in the 1840s a method of vulcanizing rubber was developed which made them both cheap and dependable.

They soon became popular – but not solely for their contraceptive properties. In Victorian times, VD was rife, largely because of prostitution. Referred to as 'the Great Social Evil', the *Westminster Review* in 1850 estimated that there were at least 8,000 girls working in London and 50,000 in the rest of the country. Mayhew's fourth volume of *London Labour and the London Poor* showed that this was a gross underestimate – there were 80,000 prostitutes in the capital alone.

Women's health and their lives were threatened, not only by their husbands' philandering, but also by the constant child-bearing that they endured. The large Victorian family was sometimes unwanted and often led to great financial hardship and poverty. The advent of the condom was a godsend.

However, the discussion of such things in public was strictly taboo. Queen Victoria would certainly not have been amused if she had ever seen a condom box. The manufacturers used pictures of the Queen and Mr Gladstone on their boxes, to recommend the product to upright Victorians. But this certainly did not commend their use to the Prince of Wales.

In the latter part of 1875, another scandal almost erupted. During the last weeks of a royal tour of India, the Prince of Wales's companion, Lord Aylesford, received a letter from his wife telling him she was about to elope with the Marquis of Blandford. Comforted by the Prince's sympathy and his denunciation of Blandford as 'the greatest blackguard alive', Aylesford returned immediately to England where he decided to sue for divorce.

Horrified, the families of Lady Aylesford and Bland-ford tried to persuade the lovers that a scandal must be avoided at all costs. But Lord Aylesford was utterly determined to go ahead with the divorce, so Blandford's brother, Randolph Churchill, appealed to the Prince of Wales to use his influence to stop the proceedings.

However, the Prince had himself enjoyed an affair with Lady Aylesford in the past, and as usual, had written her a good many compromising letters. When he refused to get involved, Churchill threatened to make the correspondence public.

He visited Princess Alexandra, informed her of her husband's infidelity and warned of the consequences to his future as King if he failed to co-operate. Edward was outraged and challenged Churchill to a duel on the north coast of France. Duels were illegal and Churchill dismissed the challenge as bravado. The idea was ridiculous, he said, as the Prince well knew.

Once again, the Queen gave her son her full support. So did Alexandra, who met the Prince's ship at sea, off the Isle of Wight, when he returned from India in May 1876.

That same evening, the Prince and Princess attended a Verdi opera at Covent Garden. Their public appearance as a happy and united couple was greeted with a lot of enthusiastic cheers and applause. Next day, the Prince received the welcome news that Lord Aylesford had decided to drop his plans for a divorce.

About a year later, when Bertie was thirty-six years old, the Arctic explorer Sir Allen Young invited him to a small supper party. The purpose of the evening was to introduce him to an attractive, twenty-three-year-old clergyman's daughter, whose name was Lillie Langtry.

Lillie had been born on the island of Jersey, the daughter of the Very Reverend William Corbert le Breton. She described her father as 'a damned nuisance', who 'could not be trusted with any woman anywhere'. Indeed, he had warned her off one of her first boyfriends in case she committed incest – the lad was one of the many wild oats that the Reverend had sown in his youth.

When she was twenty, Lillie was captivated by the spectacle of a beautiful yacht sailing into St Peter Port harbour. 'To become mistress of the yacht, I married the owner,' she later confessed. He was Edward Langtry, heir to the Belfast shipyards.

The marriage was a disaster. Langtry was a passionless man; all he felt for her was a seething jealousy. When other men would compliment her on her glowing beauty, he would reply: 'Oh, you should have seen my first wife.'

After three years of marriage, they arrived in London and the tall, violet-eyed Lillie was soon one of the most sought-after women on the social scene. The Prince of Wales was immediately captivated by her voluptuous figure.

Princess Alexandra was in Greece at the time and, when she returned, Mrs Langtry had already become Edward's mistress. Although he had always tried to be discreet about his affairs with women in the past, the Prince made no attempt to hide his infatuation with 'the Jersey Lillie'. When invited to spend the weekend at a large country house, he made it plain that he would only come if she was invited too.

They dined together several times a week and excited crowds often saw him riding by her side in Hyde Park.

He took her to Paris, where he caused a scandal by kissing her in full view of everyone on the dance-floor at Maxim's. They also made regular appearances together at Ascot, and he even managed to arrange for both her and her husband to be presented to the Queen.

'There is nothing whatever between the Prince of Wales and Lillie Langtry,' declared one newspaper, 'not even a sheet.'

Lillie was something new in the Prince's life. She was his openly-acknowledged mistress, tolerated and accepted even by Alexandra herself. This gave her a very special status, and she became an admired and important figure in her own right. In fact, within weeks of her first liaison with Bertie, she was a fêted celebrity and public figure. Even grand old society figures like Lady Cadogan were standing on chairs to catch a glimpse of her at large receptions.

'It became risky for me to indulge in a walk,' Lillie boasted later. 'People ran after me in droves, staring me out of countenance and even lifting my shade to satisfy their curiosity.'

Conscious of her position as official mistress, Lillie had her negligées trimmed with ermine. But the Prince of Wales still found it impossible to be faithful, even to her.

When the actress Sarah Bernhardt, the 'Divine Sarah', came to London, the Prince of Wales became one of her most ardent admirers. She was 'a woman of notorious, shameless character', Lady Cavendish noted in her diary. Sarah herself boasted in old age: 'I have been one of the great lovers of my century.'

The Prince's attentions soon interrupted her work as an actress. 'I've just come back from the Prince of

Wales,' she wrote in a hastily scribbled note to her director. 'It is twenty past one and I can't rehearse any more at this hour. The Prince has kept me since eleven.'

Lillie accepted such infidelities and never made a scene. The Prince's affair with her lasted for five very happy years. Finally, it was the birth of her daughter, Jeanne-Marie, in 1881 that heralded the end of their romance.

For some time, there had been rumours that she was involved with other men and Prince Louis of Battenberg was said to be the father of the child. She also became implicated in a particularly scandalous divorce case. With this, her royal affair had to come to an end.

Discarded royal mistresses were supposed to fade quietly into the background, but Lillie was made of sterner stuff. She was soon in the limelight once again – this time as an actress.

The Prince of Wales did all he could to help her prosper in her career. He persuaded Sir Squire Bancroft, the manager of the Haymarket Theatre, to back her debut in a charity performance of *She Stoops to Conquer*. His presence at the first night ensured her success and he stayed for the midnight supper she had arranged in his honour.

But her private life did not go well. The ambitious Prince Louis of Battenberg, father of Lord Mountbatten and the great-uncle of the current Duke of Edinburgh, dropped her when he found he could not marry her. Lillie went on to greater stage success in America where she received proposals from several millionaires, and slept with dozens more. Asked why she put up with the attentions of multi-millionaire George Baird, who was a

187

brutal sadist, she replied: 'I detest him, but every time he does it, he gives me a cheque for five hundred pounds.'

When Edward Langtry died a broken man – both emotionally and financially – Lillie married Baron Hugo de Bathe. She became estranged from her daughter and died in Monaco in 1929.

At forty, Bertie's sexual energies showed absolutely no signs of flagging. At the end of his affair with Lillie, he resumed his old pattern of private philandering and expeditions to the Continent for sexual adventures in Paris, the spas and other holiday resorts. Like the current Prince of Wales, he was a man without a proper role. The Queen was so determined to keep him out of affairs of state that she refused to let him take so much as a peek inside the red dispatch boxes.

Although he was given the rank of field marshall, Victoria prevented Edward from joining the British expedition to Egypt, when Arabi Pasha was defeated at the battle of Tel-el-Kebir. This irked him as many of his friends were reaping military glory there and one of his brothers, Prince Arthur, Duke of Connaught, commanded the battalion of Guards that marched on Cairo from Port Said.

Then suddenly, at forty-nine, for the very first time in his life, the Prince of Wales fell deeply and hopelessly in love. The object of his affections was Frances Brooke, or Daisy as she was known. She was twenty-nine when their affair started, strikingly beautiful, intelligent, spirited and extremely rich.

Unlike Lillie, she was an aristocrat and felt entirely at home with the Prince's social circle. Her magnificent wedding to Lord Brooke, at the age of eighteen, had been celebrated in Westminster Abbey. Prince Leopold was best man and the Prince and Princess of Wales were guests of honour. The marriage was a love match and 'Brookie' continued to show great affection for her, even after her unquenchable sexual appetite drove her to seek satisfaction with other men.

The Prince of Wales fell for Daisy after she sought his help when her affair with his friend, Lord Charles Beresford, looked set to turn into a very distasteful public scandal. Daisy and Charles had been very much in love and had sworn to be faithful. So when Lord Charles's wife fell pregnant, Daisy was furious. She wrote a scalding letter to her lover. Out it fell into his wife's hands and she, in turn, threatened to use it to ruin Daisy.

'He was more than kind,' she later wrote about her meeting with the Prince, 'and suddenly I saw him looking at me in a way all women understand.' The Prince of Wales used his influence to hush up the matter and Daisy was, of course, only too eager to show her gratitude. 'He was a very perfect, gentle lover,' she wrote. 'Anyone would have been won by him.'

In Daisy, Bertie was dealing with a woman of independence and character – a woman who wouldn't always let him have the upper hand. She had a passion for hunting, driving a four-in-hand and giving the sort of house parties where there was much to-ing and fro-ing between the bedrooms.

The etiquette was strict. Husbands and wives were given separate bedrooms. If a woman was willing to take a lover to her room, she would pick up a silver candlestick before going to bed. This would give her admirer the excuse to light it for her and whisper the suggestion of an assignation. Otherwise, a note would be passed from his valet to her maid. Lovers would leave something outside the door to show that the coast was clear. Sandwiches on a plate were used as a signal until the gluttonous German diplomat, Baron von Eckardstein, was found eating them.

Partners would return to their own rooms at 6 am. Next day, they would give no hint that they had spent the night together.

Naturally, these arrangements could sometimes go wrong. At one house party, Lord Charles Beresford crept along the landing into the wrong room, leaped on the bed shouting 'cock-a-doodle-doo', only to find himself in between the Bishop of Chester and his wife. He left the house before breakfast.

Daisy had a reckless streak and loved the thrill of danger – she once drove her coach 300 miles non-stop, from her house in Easton to Land's End, just to admire the view. She was also among the first people to try one of the new fangled-bicycles. The high drama and excitement of an affair with the Prince of Wales suited her perfectly and she entered into it with all her natural gusto. The Prince was bowled over.

From the beginning of 1891, he was a regular visitor to Easton Lodge. This contained a pretty summer house secreted in the grounds, which was a favourite meeting place for the two lovers. There they exchanged rings, after which he called her: 'My own adored Daisy wife'. Daisy even had a station built near to the house, so the Prince could reach her quicker on his own private train.

As time passed, the Prince became less cautious about appearing with Daisy in public. He accompanied her to church and often took her out to dine at one of London's fashionable restaurants – Rules in Maiden Lane, the Café Royal and Kettner's were among their favourites. And, when they were apart, he wrote her long impassioned letters two or three times a week.

In 1894 Daisy's father-in-law, the Earl of Warwick, died and she became the Countess of Warwick. She inherited Warwick Castle and a huge fortune. At around the same time, she fell under the influence of W.T. Stead, a newspaper editor and an early socialist. Excited by his idealism, she soon embraced socialism as passionately as she had always embraced everything else.

When the royal romance finally began to fade, it was due as much to Daisy's increasing commitment to politics as to her involvement with other men. Edward soon began carrying on with various other ladies and, after 1896, their relationship became increasingly platonic. It ended completely in 1898 with the birth of her son, Maynard. But she always retained a special place in the Prince's heart and he continued to write to her until his death in 1910.

In later years, Edward also did his best to make peace between his ex-mistress and his wife. He showed Alexandra a letter in which Daisy had called her an 'angel of goodness'.

In his reply he said of Alexandra: 'She really, quite forgives and condones the past, as I have corroborated what you wrote about our friendship having been platonic for some years. You could not help, my loved one, writing to me as you did – though it gave me a pang – after the letters I have received from you for nearly nine years!'

However, after his death, Daisy ran up debts amounting to £100,000 and, with the aid of notorious journalist Frank Harris, let it be known that she was about to publish her royal letters. George V immediately took her to court, claiming that the palace held the copyright and the matter was buried for the next fifty years.

The Prince of Wales met Mrs Keppel in February 1898, the year his relationship with Daisy ended. Immediately, he was captivated. The same month, he met another woman to whom he was powerfully attracted – Agnes Keyser.

The two women could not have been more different. Alice was married to George Keppel, the son of the seventh Earl of Albermarle. She was a bright, voluptuous twenty-nine-year-old beauty, who had made her mark in fashionable circles. The writer Sir Osbert Sitwell found her a delightful conversationalist and described how 'she would remove from her mouth for a moment the cigarette which she would be smoking through a long holder and turn upon the person to whom she was speaking her large, humorous, kindly, peculiarly discerning eyes'.

Alice's husband was a tall, dashing army officer with the good looks of a matinée idol. He was very fond of the ladies himself and, although he loved his wife dearly, he seemed to feel that accommodating her affair with the King was his patriotic duty. As time passed, he grew to feel a genuine affection for the old libertine. When their money ran out – due largely to Alice's extravagance – George happily went to work for Sir Thomas Lipton, at the King's instigation.

Agnes Keyser, on the other hand, was a handsome forty-six-year-old spinster. She had the warm, strong

personality of a kindly governess and a strident voice
that carried all too powerfully down even long corridors.
She was the daughter of a wealthy stockbroker, who ran
a nursing home for army officers in London's Grosvenor Crescent. This was supported, in part, by donations
from the Prince's rich friends.

Agnes bossed the Prince of Wales about and fussed
over her royal suitor as nobody else had ever dared to.
She had little contact with society and entertained him
quietly in the comfortable, furnished rooms of her
apartment on the top floor of the hospital. Sometimes
they played draughts and she frequently warned him of
the dangers to his health of overeating. At Miss Keyser's
table Bertie was served only the plainest food – Irish
stews and bland milk puddings.

Strong though his attachment to Agnes Keyser was, it
lacked the sexual ingredient necessary to make it last.
Instead, it was Alice Keppel who became the woman
who would love Bertie and be loved by him for the
remainder of his life.

The initial spark was sexual attraction, but Alice soon
showed herself to have the precise qualities required to
be the mistress of an ageing king. Kind, amusing, intelligent and discreet, she was the royal 'friend' *par
excellence*. She kept him entertained and in good temper.

The Prince of Wales came to the throne when he was
nearly sixty. By then he was fat and balding, with forty
years of gluttony, gambling and carousing behind him.
He abandoned his father's name – Albert – and reigned
as Edward VII.

The new king systematically moved his mother's property into storage rooms at Windsor and destroyed Prince

Albert's rooms which had been preserved like a shrine since his death. He also defied his mother's will by giving the family house, Osborne, to the Royal Navy as a training college.

The Coronation was arranged for 26th June, but Edward became ill and almost died of peritonitis, so the ceremony had to be postponed. The vast quantities of specially prepared food could not go to waste, so 2,500 quails, 300 legs of mutton, oysters, prawns, snipe, consommé de faisan aux quenelles and sole poached in Chablis were distributed among the poor of London's East End. By the time the King was eventually crowned on 9th August, he had risen in popular esteem from a worthless wastrel to the most popular monarch since Charles II.

At the coronation in Westminster Abbey, a box above the chancel was reserved for the King's mistresses. This was referred to coyly as 'The King's loose-box'.

It housed Sarah Bernhardt, Lady Kilmorey, Mrs Hartmann, Mrs Paget and Mrs Alice Keppel among others. Henry James, the American writer who later became a British citizen, was more direct when he called the new King 'the arch vulgarian, Edward the Caresser'.

Mrs Keppel was soon installed as the *maîtresse en titre*. Hostesses inviting the King for a country weekend would make sure that she was on the guest list as well. Everybody, including her accommodating husband, adored her.

She ruffled no feathers and seemed to be immune to malicious gossip. Even Alexandra was grateful for the good influence that she exercised over her husband and she was the only one of the King's mistresses to be

regularly invited to both Marlborough House and Sandringham.

Alice could also be relied upon for her discretion and
was often used by the government as an intermediary
with Edward. Lord Hardinge of Penshurst, Viceroy of
India, noted: 'There were one or two occasions when
the King was in disagreement with the Foreign Office,
and I was able, through her, to advise the King with a
view to the policy of the government being accepted.'

The royal couple and the Keppels were often invited
to the same parties. A few – such as the Duke of Port-
land, the Marquis of Salisbury and the Duke of Norfolk
– looked down their noses at her. But out of mischief,
the King would sometimes seat the Archbishop of Canterbury next to Mrs Keppel.

Despite his age, Edward was as promiscuous as ever.
He maintained regular liaisons with several married
society ladies and spent the summer, as always, in Paris
or Marienbad. Mrs Keppel was never jealous or possessive. Like Alexandra, she learned to tolerate his infidelity.

They spent each Easter in Biarritz. There they enjoyed long walks together, gambled at the casino, or just
stayed in, playing bridge. Once the King chided Mrs
Keppel when she miscalled. She responded that she was
sorry but she could never 'tell a King from a Knave'.

Despite the demands of State, Edward and Mrs Keppel were never separated for long. They were constantly
weekending together and he was a frequent and welcome visitor at the Keppels' elegant town house in
Portman Square. Her two young daughters regarded
him as a rather grand uncle and were even allowed the

liberty of racing slices of buttered toast down his immaculate trouser legs.

In 1910, Edward VII suffered a series of heart attacks and it soon became clear that he was dying. As the situation worsened, someone informed Alexandra that Mrs Keppel, who had left the King's side the previous day, was not due to return again until the following afternoon.

'It will be too late,' the Queen replied. She gave orders that her husband's mistress should be sent for immediately.

After the King's death, the Keppels' house was plunged into deep mourning. One of his daughters asked George tearfully: 'Why does it matter so much Kingy dying?' To which the generous-hearted cuckold replied: 'Because Kingy was a very, very wonderful person.'

Edward VII should have been succeeded by his son Eddy, who was a homosexual. At Cambridge, the Prince had an intense affair with his tutor James Stephen, who went mad after Eddy left him to join the 10th Hussars.

The Prince was also a member of the notorious Hundred Guineas Club in Cleveland Street, where he was known as Victoria. His membership of the club led him to be implicated in the infamous 'Cleveland Street Scandal' over the running of a male brothel on the premises.

The Prince's dissolute reputation has caused some researchers to suggest that Eddy was Jack the Ripper. Others believe he was involved in the murder of a baby he fathered by a prostitute.

Eddy had at least two heterosexual affairs before his betrothal to Princess Mary of Teck. But before the wedding could take place, Eddy was struck down by what was said to be pneumonia but was probably syphilis, contracted from a prostitute. He died before he could succeed to the throne.

Eddy's younger brother George had been brought up in the same nursery and the two children were treated as twins. As young men, both of them joined the Navy together. They even shared the same mistress in St John's Wood. She was a 'ripper', according to Prince George. As a dashing young naval officer, he also kept a mistress in Southsea, which was conveniently close to the naval base at Portsmouth.

But George was as inhibited as Eddy had been carefree. He was a strict disciplinarian with a deep fixation on his mother, whom he often referred to as 'dear, sweet, loving, beloved little Mother dear'. Despite his obvious devotion, Princess Alexandra chided him for bringing on her 'the sad disgrace of being the mother of a dwarf'. He measured only five foot seven.

Queen Victoria tried to marry him off to the fifteen-year-old 'Missy', Princess Marie of Edinburgh, in whose company he had spent a great deal of his time when he was in Malta. However, she chose King Ferdinand of Rumania instead.

Then he had a tragic love affair with Sir Robert Peel's granddaughter Julie Sonor, but she was a Catholic as well as a commoner. Although they were deeply in love, marriage was ruled impossible under the Act of Settlement. Nevertheless, they remained lifelong friends.

Eventually, George was coerced into marrying his dead brother's fiancée, Princess Mary of Teck. This spelled the sudden end of George's romantic dreams. 'I only wish that you could marry and be happy,' Princess Alexandra, told her son, 'but, alas, I fear it cannot be.'

Indeed, the match was loveless. After their marriage, lady-in-waiting Lady Geraldine Somerset wrote: 'It is clear there is not even the pretence of love-making.'

This was far removed from the music hall joke of the time in which, on the morning after their wedding, Mary asks George whether the common people do 'that'. George replies that he believes they do. 'Well, it shouldn't be allowed,' she replied, 'It's too good for them.'

Marriage had changed nothing, his mother chillingly wrote: 'There is a bond of love between us, that of mother and child, which nobody can ever diminish or render less binding – and nobody can, or ever shall, come between me and my darling Georgie boy.'

Like dutiful royals, however, Mary and George performed their function and produced six children – one of whom, John, was an epileptic and was seldom included in family portraits. He lived apart from the family, in the care of a nanny for most of his fourteen years. He died in 1919.

Outside sailing and slaughtering small birds, George V had only one hobby. He collected every issue of British Empire stamps. Each of these bore his own portrait. A noted psychologist has suggested that, in this solitary pastime, he was in fact playing with himself.

During the First World War, George banned alcohol from the court, and ladies-in-waiting were never allowed to wear the fashionable short skirts that showed an inch or two of leg. 'In court circles,' the directive went, 'ankle bones are not to be countenanced.'

Queen Mary was little better. She said she found childbirth a 'complete violation of one's feelings'.

On 7th July 1917, after a daylight bombing raid on London by 24 German Gotha bombers, which killed forty-four Britons and injured 125 more, a mob rioted, attacking German-owned property. George V decided that it was time to change the royal family's name, anglicizing it from Saxe-Coburg-Gotha to something more suitable – Windsor.

This was achieved with a minimum of fuss and George V went on to live a blameless and uneventful life, marked by only the slightest hint of scandal. At the time of his accession, court action had to be taken to scotch the widespread rumour that he had been married to May, the daughter of Admiral Culme-Seymour, before his marriage to Queen Mary.

When the rumour was published in a republican newspaper called the *Liberator*, the editor, E. F. Mylius, was prosecuted. The trial was heard in front of the Lord Chief Justice, who refused to allow the defence to sub-poena the King himself. Mylius was found guilty and sentenced to a year in prison. When he was released, he repeated the libel in America, but no further action was taken.

The Attorney General, Sir Rufus Isaacs, and the Solicitor General, Sir John Simmon, who handled the case were both decorated with the Royal Victorian Order by the grateful sovereign. Sir John Simmon went on to be the Foreign Secretary and Lord Chancellor. Sir Rufus Isaacs, later Lord Reading, became Lord Chief Justice and Viceroy of India, despite well-founded allegations of insider-dealing at the Marconi Company.

There were rumours, too, that George had consorted with seaside prostitutes. It was also said that he had had an affair with Queen Maria Cristina, the widow of Spain's King Alfonso XII. This was supposed to have resulted in the birth of an illegitimate daughter, Helle Cristina Habsburg Windsor, who lived in Malta until her death in 1990, at the ripe old age of a hundred.

13

THE GREATEST LOVE STORY EVER TOLD

Edward VIII's decision to abdicate so that he could marry Wallis Simpson is said to have been one of the greatest love stories ever told. But was it? The allegation has been made that his obsession with her was purely sexual.

In his youth, the Prince of Wales bore a striking resemblance to his grandfather Edward VII. But when David – as the Prince was known – was instructed about sex in his late teens by the Reverend Wright, he wrote to a friend saying that he had never been troubled with the 'sexual hunger'.

During the First World War, the Prince was taken to a brothel in Calais where, it is said, he found the sight of the prostitutes 'perfectly filthy and revolting'. He had his first sexual experience in Amiens, then took up with a courtesan in Paris. Perhaps there was Hanoverian blood in his veins after all. He was also unwise enough to write to the girl and these letters led to a brief blackmail panic.

Back in London he courted Lady Sybil Cadogan, before falling in love with Marian Coke, a married woman twelve years his senior. Other affairs followed, mainly with married women. One of these involvements was with Freda Dudley Ward, the divorced wife of an MP. They met during a Zeppelin raid when she ran for cover to a house where he was a party guest.

The affair lasted a couple of years, but the Prince was not faithful. There were always plenty of wives and daughters ready to accommodate the desires of the heir to the throne. He had a brief relationship with Audrey James, the daughter of an American industrialist. She seems to have repulsed his advances while single, but after she married they had a 'merry little caper together – merry but brief'.

When Audrey's sexual interest waned, Edward took up with Lady Thelma Furness. She was the daughter of an American diplomat, who had eloped at sixteen with a man twice her age. They were soon divorced and Thelma went on to marry Viscount Furness, a shipping magnate infamous for his love of brandy and women. Thelma joined the Prince in Kenya in 1928 where, under the African sky, they felt 'as if we were the only two people in the world'.

Romantically, Lady Thelma recorded in her journal: 'This was our Eden, and we were alone in it. His arms about me were the only reality; his words of love my only bridge to life. Borne along on the mounting tide of his ardour, I felt myself being inexorably swept from the accustomed moorings of caution. Every night I felt more completely possessed by our love.'

But later, when the spark had gone out of the affair, she complained that he was very poorly endowed and a lacklustre sexual performer. Cruelly she, and many others, called him 'The Little Man'. At the naval college at Osborne, the Prince was known as 'Sardine' rather than 'Whales'.

On her way back to England after a trip to New York, Thelma met the notorious playboy Aly Khan, the son of the Aga Khan. He had been sent to Cairo at the age of eighteen by his father to be trained by the madams of the great bordellos in the Imsak, the art of withholding ejaculation. It was said that, like Father Christmas, Aly came only once a year.

The Prince of Wales immediately dropped Thelma. He was a shameless racist. On a trip to South Africa in 1925, he had refused to dance with any of the black women attending an official reception, when his ship put in at Sierra Leone, declaring: 'It really is too much.'

Edward may even have had homosexual tendencies. The homosexual writer Lytton Strachey mentioned how he had eyed up an 'attractive tart – fair-haired this time' in the Tate Gallery, only to discover that this was the Prince of Wales. 'I fled – perhaps foolishly,' he wrote. 'Perhaps it might have been the beginning of a really entertaining affair.'

Meanwhile, Thelma's place in the Prince of Wales's bed had already been taken by her best friend, Wallis Simpson. She was an American, born in Baltimore of rich Virginian stock. Her first husband had been a navy flier called Lieutenant Earl Winfield 'Win' Spencer. He was an alcoholic who had enjoyed several extra-marital affairs with both men and women. With Wallis, he had acted like a jealous sadist. He would frequently tie her to the bed and beat her.

For her own part, Wallis had carried on affairs with the Italian Ambassador, Prince Gelasio Caetani, and an Argentine diplomat, Felipe Espil, who was said to dance the best tango in Washington.

Travelling through China in the 1920s, Wallis had visited houses of prostitution with names like the 'Fields of Glittering Flowers' and the 'Clubs of Ducks and Mandarins'. There were also the luxurious 'flower boats' where one could enjoy both a splendid meal and exotic, sexual entertainments devised by experts in the erotic arts. There she was taught 'perverse practices'. These included watching lesbian displays and partaking in a threesome without her husband. She also learned Fang Chung, an Ancient Chinese erotic art. This is a method of relaxing the male partner through pro-longed and carefully modulated hot oil massage of the nipples, stomach, thighs and, after cruelly protracted delay, the genitals. Devotees of Fang Chung are taught the location of the main nerve centres and the methods of delicately brushing the skin to arouse even the most passionless of men.

The technique was also useful for men who suffered from premature ejaculation. Firm pressure between the urethra and the anus could prevent a man coming almost indefinitely. According to a close friend, Wallis had no sooner learned these techniques than her first husband Win left her to move in with a handsome young painter.

In Shanghai, she enjoyed a 'delightful friendship' with a young American called Robbie, while in Peking she began a long-term relationship with Herman Rogers, another wealthy American. There were also rumours that Wallis had been involved in a lesbian affair with Mrs Mary Sadler, the wife of Admiral F. H. Sadler. In addition, it was said that Wallis, Herman Rogers and his wife Katherine had joined in a *ménage à trois*. Further reports alleged that she was involved in drug peddling.

Wallis certainly had affairs with the Italian naval attaché, Aberto de Zara and Count Galeazzo Ciano, later Mussolini's Foreign Minister. She became pregnant by Ciano and the subsequent botched abortion left her unable to have children.

Wallis eventually returned to America. In New York she met Ernest Simpson, a British citizen, and began a torrid affair with him. Neither of them was single, but they hastily organized their respective divorces, married and moved to London.

But married life changed nothing. Wallis went on a women-only trip to the south of France with Consuela Thaw and Gloria Vanderbilt, who at the time was having a lesbian affair with Nada. Wallis shared a room with Consuela, but that did not stop her going out hunting for eligible men.

Wallis Simpson and the Prince of Wales mixed in the same circles and, as Thelma Furness's best friend, it was inevitable that they should run across one another.

In 1934, the Prince of Wales was supposed to have fathered two illegitimate sons – one by the younger sister of an old flame and another who was christened Anthony Chisholm and was the Prince's own godson. But by 1935, George V was accusing the Prince of keeping Wallis as a mistress. Edward denied this indignantly, even though servants at his home at Fort Belvedere had seen the two of them in bed together.

According to one friend, the techniques that Wallis had learned in China did not entirely overcome the

Prince's extreme lack of virility that Thelma Furness was talking so openly about by then. It is doubtful whether he and Wallis ever actually had sexual intercourse in the normal sense of the word. However, she did manage to give him relief. Edward had always been a repressed foot-fetishist, and once she had discovered this, Wallis indulged his fantasy completely.

They also became involved in elaborate erotic games, including nanny–child scenes, in which she was dominant, he happily submissive. By satisfying these needs – needs he had probably never even expressed before – Wallis earned his everlasting gratitude and knew that he would depend on her for a lifetime. It was enough to make any man give up the throne.

However it may just have been that the Prince suffered from an extreme form of premature ejaculation, and that Wallis introduced him to techniques that overcame the problem. There have also been rumours that she had an operation to tighten her vagina, an act much appreciated by the Prince, and she was probably an expert at fellatio.

Edward and Mrs Simpson belonged to a fast set. While she was entertaining the Prince of Wales, her husband Ernest had embarked on an affair with Mary Raffray. The four of them became a flagrant *ménage à quatre*. But Wallis still had outside interests. While Nazi Germany was invading the Rhineland, Wallis was said to be having an affair with the German Ambassador, von Ribbentrop.

It is clear from her letters that Wallis did not love the Prince of Wales. She enjoyed her power over him. One day, in front of friends she commanded: 'Take off my dirty shoes and bring me another pair.' To everyone's astonishment, he knelt down and did as he was told. Freda Dudley Ward said: 'He made himself the slave of whomsoever he loved, and became totally dependent on her. It was his nature: he was like a masochist. He liked being humbled, degraded. He begged for it.'

When the Prince of Wales became King, he decided to reign under the name of Edward, like his notorious grandfather, rather than his Christian name David. However, he also knew that he could not do without his Wallis and so was determined to make her his wife.

A divorce was speedily arranged for Mrs Simpson. For the convenience of Wallis and the King, Ernest was found in a hotel bedroom with Buttercup Kennedy. He is said to have regretted that he had only one wife to lay down for his King.

Edward and Mrs Simpson set off on a Mediterranean cruise. While establishment pressure had managed to keep news of the affair out of the British press, the American papers were hailing 'Queen Wally' in what they claimed to be the biggest story of the century. In Britain, the impending royal nuptials became a matter for political concern. Prime Minister Stanley Baldwin argued that the British people would never stand for it.

'Why shouldn't the King marry his cutie?' blustered Churchill.

'Because England does not want a Queen Cutie,' answered Noël Coward.

When the crisis finally broke in the British press, Mrs Simpson fled to France and offered to 'withdraw' from the situation. But the King would not have it. On 11th December 1936, he abdicated, having reigned for less than a year.

How typical of him, one wit commented, to give up the position of Admiral of the Fleet in order to be third mate on a Baltimore tramp.

When she heard the news while lunching at the Ritz, Alice Keppel said: 'Things were done better in my day.'

As Duke of Windsor, Edward VIII went into permanent exile with Mrs Simpson. Although they married, his brother and heir George VI refused to grant the Duchess the title of Her Royal Highness and prevented the couple from ever returning again to England.

Edward VIII, it is said, gave up everything for the woman he loved. However, in the 1950s, it was reported that she had grown tired of his cloying affections and was having a very public affair with New York playboy Jimmy Donahue, the heir to the Woolworth fortune.

In fact, Jimmy Donahue was a notorious homosexual. His father before him had been gay and had committed suicide when his lover, a young serviceman, jilted him.

Press agents fought to photograph Donahue arm in arm with beautiful, publicity-seeking women, but he was exclusively homosexual. He staged elaborate orgies with rent boys in his family home and was a close friend of Cardinal Spellman, whose affairs with male prostitutes and pretty young Catholic priests had already scandalized New York. It was said that Spellman had turned up to one of Donahue's parties wearing a ballgown.

In 1947, when Donahue was introduced to the Duke and Duchess of Windsor, it is said that the Duke was strongly attracted to him and that, within a year, they were involved in a torrid affair. To cover their tracks, Donahue flirted publicly with the Duchess while the Duke pretended to despise all homosexuals. Others say that Wallis was genuinely having an affair with Donahue, in an attempt to make him heterosexual.

Noël Coward, who became a close friend of the Windsors after the abdication, summed the situation up in the following way: 'I like Jimmy. He's an insane camp but he's fun. I like the Duchess; she's a fag hag to end all fag hags, but that's what makes her likeable. The Duke ... well, although he pretends not to hate me, he does because I'm queer and he's queer. However, unlike him I don't pretend not to be. Here she's got a royal queen to sleep with and a rich one to hump.'

After a short break, Donahue and the Duke and Duchess of Windsor travelled together, but the curious *ménage à trois* foundered, partly because of Donahue's growing entourage of rent boys and partly because of his passion for garlic. Neither the Duke nor the Duchess could abide the smell of it on his breath.

George VI succeeded his brother Edward VIII. He was painfully shy and suffered from a terrible stammer. His character, like that of Edward VIII, seems to have been formed largely by their neurotic nanny, who doted on David while neglecting Albert, the future King George. She would pinch the young Prince of Wales to make him scream, so that Queen Mary would order her to take him back to the nursery, and she ruined the Duke of York's digestion by not feeding him properly. Eventually, as a result of overwork – she was never allowed any holidays by the royal parents – the Prince's nanny had a nervous breakdown and was dismissed.

While the Prince of Wales did everything he could to upset his father, the Duke of York always tried to please George V, and even took his name when he came to the throne.

Although a commoner, Elizabeth Bowes-Lyon was originally introduced to the Prince of Wales in the hope that they might make an early marriage. Initially, he took little notice of her and she 'knew what she wanted and that was absolute purity'. Despite this, the shy young Albert eventually coaxed her into marriage, after proposing to her three times before she gave her consent.

The Duke of York never expected to accede to the throne. He certainly could not have anticipated the abdication crisis, nor the possibility of becoming the figurehead of a nation when it was involved in total war. Indeed, his main interest before reluctantly taking the throne was in running the Duke of York's camps, where slum boys and pupils from public schools could meet and mix freely.

George was a heavy smoker and died of lung cancer in 1952. In the latter part of his life, smoking may also have made him impotent. He also suffered from Buerger's disease. This results in poor circulation to the legs and, almost certainly, a restriction in the blood supply to the penis, causing erectile impotence.

While George VI was stuffy and strait-laced, his younger brother Prince George, the Duke of Kent, displayed a much more hedonistic attitude to life. In the 1930s he had had affairs with a succession of society girls and was believed to have discussed marriage with at least two of them, Lois Stuart and Poppy Baring.

The then Prince of Wales introduced George to the theatrical set and he fell in with a homosexual crowd. He was said to have had affairs with an Argentine diplomat, an Italian aristocrat, Noël Coward and Sir Malcolm Sargent.

There was also talk of a scandal concerning some letters that he had written to a young man in Paris. A large sum of money had to be paid in order to retrieve them. And, on one occasion, he was arrested in a dubious nightclub called the Nut House. He spent several hours in the cells before his identity could be established.

The Prince experimented with cocaine, the fashionable drug of the 1930s. Even the Prince of Wales was familiar with this white powder. Often, it would be passed around in the Muthaiga Club in his presence and snorted just before the loyal toast. George was also introduced to morphine by a young American girl called Kiki Whitney Preston.

George eventually did what was expected of him. He married a royal princess, Marina. She had links with both the Greek and Russian royal families, and was tolerant and comfortable around homosexuals. Indeed, after George died in a wartime aircrash, she took as her lover Danny Kaye, who had himself enjoyed a homosexual affair with the Prince.

When George VI died prematurely, his widow, the Queen Mother, was just fifty-two. She is known to be a tremendously fun-loving woman and over the last forty years numerous men have expressed an interest in her.

One of the reasons for this must be her lively sense of humour. One evening at the cocktail hour, when the Queen Mother could get no response from her bell, she stormed downstairs to find two of her footmen arguing.

'Perhaps when you two old queens have finished quarrelling, you'll bring this old queen a gin and tonic,' was her tart remark. And when one of her servants was arrested for 'cottaging' in a public lavatory, she sent an official car for him with a bunch of flowers and a note saying: 'Naughty boy!'

In 1990, the Queen Mother even let it slip that she had, indeed, been in love with the Prince of Wales before the abdication crisis.

14

GOOD QUEEN BESS

Despite the shocking antics of their ancestors, the current royal family appear to have led blameless lives. They have always acted with total discretion and, until the republican newspaper magnate Rupert Murdoch arrived in Britain, the newspapers remained respectful and neglected to mention any royal peccadillo. The foreign press, however, has always made the most of any scandalous gossip they could get hold of about the royals.

Of course it would be treasonable to make any suggestions about the Queen. Even though her name has occasionally been linked romantically with that of her racing manager, Lord Porchester, no one actually believes such a scurrilous rumour. Nevertheless, it is really not that difficult to get into her bedroom, as the disturbed burglar, Michael Fagan, proved in 1982.

During the investigation that followed the break-in, it was revealed that gay bed-hopping had occurred in the servants' quarters at Buckingham Palace. Drugs were also freely available and there had been wild parties. After official banquets, there would often be a free-for-all as servants scrambled for the left-over food and wine. Sometimes there would be a race to sit in the Queen's chair and give orders. After one particularly long shift, one of the palace waitresses whipped off her top in an impromptu striptease.

In addition, a number of servants from the Queen's household have been arrested for homosexual offences. Three were disgraced after holding a gay orgy in one of the Palace's huge enamel baths. Even the Queen's eighty-three-year-old Clerk of the Royal Kitchens was recently ensnared by the *News of the World* when he was with a hooker.

Prince Philip was born in Greece, but his roots are Danish and German. His uncle was expelled from the country for supporting the Germans during World War I. During the hostilities, Philip's mother was rescued by a British warship and taken to Corfu, then a British Protectorate. There, Philip was born and brought up in a villa called Mon Repos.

Philip's 'Uncle Dickie' – Lord Louis Mountbatten – had great plans for him. He intended to marry his nephew to the heir to the British throne. Philip first met Elizabeth when she was just thirteen and they soon began a regular correspondence. But, during the war, he saw a great deal of his cousin, the twenty-year-old Princess Alexandra – in Greece, Egypt and South Africa. Eventually, she turned up in London where they enjoyed a two-year relationship.

Princess Alexandra later married King Peter of Yugoslavia and spent her life in exile, while Prince Philip went on to pursue his royal courtship. During this time, he was staying with the Milford Haven family. The Marquis is renowned for his collection of pornography, kept in the library at Lynden Manor, and for his marriage to Nada, the lesbian lover of Edwina Mountbatten. The latter's many conquests included the jazz singer 'Hutch' and Pandit Nehru.

After a time, Philip moved in with 'Dickie' Mountbatten. Rumours of homosexuality surrounded the latter throughout his life. He also claimed to be the first man to have a zip sewn into the fly of his trousers. 'A minute can be as costly as an hour,' he would joke to his servants.

Mountbatten – who had already changed his name from the Germanic Battenberg – helped his nephew to become a British citizen, as Philip Mountbatten, rather than under his original name, Philip Schleswig-Holstein-Sonderburg-Glucksburg. He pointed out how Philip had served on board a British warship during the war, while playing down the fact that his sisters had all married high-ranking Nazis, one of them a Luftwaffe pilot who had bombed Britain during the conflict. Philip's father, Prince Andrew, was another embarrassment. He lived with a French widow, Madame Andrée de la Bigne, on her yacht in Monte Carlo.

Even while wooing Elizabeth, Philip was often seen without her, drinking and dancing in West End clubs. After his marriage, it was suggested that he enjoyed the company of a number of nightclub 'hostesses'. Certainly, he belonged to an informal gentleman's club that boasted among its members Dr Stephen Ward, a key figure in the Profumo scandal. The Soviet spy, Yevgeny Ivanov, who shared the favours of Christine Keeler with the Secretary of State for War, John Profumo, claims that he lodged with the Russian GRU compromising evidence that could be used against Prince Philip, and even possibly against the Queen herself.

Philip's name was also linked with the Greek singer Helene Cordet, whom he had known since adolescence and who was the mother of two illegitimate children. Similar stories circulated about the actress Anna Massey, a French cabaret star by whom he is supposed to have had a daughter named Charlotte, and the actress Pat Kirkwood. All have been denied with varying degrees of conviction.

The Queen seems to have tolerated his prolonged absences from her side. It has even been suggested that if Prince Philip did need to satisfy the sexual side of his nature elsewhere, she would accept that as part of life.

Princess Margaret's sex life has been more of an open book. As a young girl she fell for Group Captain Peter Townsend, a divorced man almost twice her age. The American papers were quick to pick up on the affair, but the British papers suppressed the story. Eventually, the *Sunday People* plucked up the courage to repeat what the foreign press had been saying for some time already. But by now, it was too late. The crucial decision had already been made.

Although Townsend had divorced his wife on the grounds of her adultery, the Palace and the government – still sensitive from the abdication crisis – were determined to prevent Princess Margaret from marrying him. One of the main critics was Prince Philip, even though Townsend had supported him during his courtship with Princess Elizabeth. So the airman was bundled off to

Belgium and, whenever he was due to return, Margaret was told that the timing was still not propitious. Eventually, she was told that when she reached the age of twenty-five, she could marry without the Queen's consent – although she would have to renounce the succession and the Civil List. By the time she reached this age, however, she had been persuaded against the match.

In her disappointment, Princess Margaret took to nightclubbing and the papers soon found other names to link with hers. One of these was Billy Wallace. Rumour had it that she was about to announce her engagement to him, when he jetted off to the Bahamas and had a wild fling with a local girl. On his return, Margaret dropped him after a vitriolic slanging match.

She was 'just good friends' with Colin Tennant, when she met and fell for the photographer Anthony Armstrong-Jones. For a time she had to share him with his live-in lover, the Oriental model Jacqui Chan. But when Margaret and Tony began holding their assignations in his shabby Rotherhithe apartment, the girl soon moved out.

Before their engagement, there had already been strong rumours about Armstrong-Jones's sexual predilections. These were revived when he invited Jeremy Fry, a legal homosexual, to be his best man. His second choice was Jeremy Thorpe.

The marriage was said to be passionate, but in 1966, while he was away on an assignment, she had an affair with one of her husband's friends, Anthony Barton, a married man with two children. After the brief fling, Princess Margaret called Barton's wife and apologized. She also told her husband.

The marriage came under increasing strain as Armstrong-Jones, created Earl of Snowdon on his marriage, was frequently away on photographic assignments. There were rumoured affairs with Dominic Elliot and Derek Hart, and she became 'kissing cousins' with the Earl of Lichfield. Margaret also had an affair with her childhood friend and popular society pianist Robin Douglas-Home, who later committed suicide.

Meanwhile, the Earl of Snowdon had an affair with twenty-two-year-old Lady Jacqueline Rufus-Isaacs, and was subsequently seen with a succession of other attractive women. In retaliation, Margaret took up with Roddy Llewellyn, a man seventeen years her junior.

The couple were pictured together on the West Indian island of Mustique and at a hippie-style commune in Wiltshire, where one of the other members of the group set up a tape-recorder outside Margaret and Roddy's door, in the hope of capturing on tape the royal 'squawk'.

Before he met Princess Margaret, Llewellyn had been sharing a flat with a gay friend. He later told his friends that he had found it very difficult to cope with the physical side of his relationship with Margaret, though this did not prevent him marrying Tania Soskin.

Princess Margaret then did the unthinkable – at least in royal circles. She put an end to her marriage, with a divorce. Lord Snowdon received a six-figure sum in settlement and, later in the same year, he married his production assistant, Lucy Lindsay-Hogg.

15

A ROYAL FLUSH

The year 1992 was indeed an *annus horribilis* for the British royal family. An intimate biography of the Princess of Wales, written apparently with her tacit consent, had revealed a deep rift between Diana and her husband Prince Charles. The flame-haired Duchess of York was photographed cavorting topless with her American financial adviser, Johnny Bryan – effectively ending her marriage to Prince Andrew. Finally, Princess Anne and Captain Mark Phillips divorced after allegations that he had fathered a love-child, the product of a one-night stand in New Zealand.

Things scarcely improved in 1993. New transcripts of intimate phone calls allegedly between Prince Charles and his long-time friend Camilla Parker-Bowles, and between Princess Diana and her putative lover James Gilbey were published. The Wales's marriage, too, was now at an end. All three marriages of the royal children had failed.

Admittedly, the fourth royal child, Prince Edward, announced his engagement, but he has been no stranger to controversy. After quitting the Royal Marines, he went to work at Andrew Lloyd Webber's Really Useful Theatre Company, where he was known as 'Barbara' Windsor, after the star of the *Carry On...* films. Despite working in the theatre, he showed little interest in show girls and repeated allegations that he is gay have been either ignored or parried, but never denied. Then, just when everything seemed to have died down, there were fresh allegations surrounding the ever-embarrassing Major Ron Ferguson, the Duchess of York's father.

Perhaps this disintegration was inevitable. Since Queen Victoria, the royal family had adopted the role of Britain's first family. They constituted the linchpin of religion, in the guise of the Church of England, the Establishment and the British class system. Throughout the nineteenth and early twentieth centuries, anything that diverged from this image of the perfect family could be contained. Compliant press lords quashed any hint of scandal. Only when matters came to open court did the British public learn anything of the excesses of Edward VII. Even Edward VIII's love affair with Mrs Simpson was kept out of the British press until the very eve of the King's abdication, although it had been widely reported abroad.

Today, however, technical advances have made the global media network impossible to control. Even though newspapers in Britain declined to publish the so-called 'Camillagate' tapes when they first fell into their hands, once the transcripts had been published by *New Idea* magazine in Australia, thousands of privately faxed copies were soon available in Britain. After that, there was no point in the press showing restraint. The tabloids printed, word for word, the romantic – and scatological – conversation, which plainly indicated that the Prince was having an intimate relationship with a married woman. The quality press devoted acres of newsprint to condemning this gross invasion of privacy, while filling their own copy full of nods and winks and innuendo.

Where had the tapes come from? Conspiracy theories abounded. MI5 was bugging the Palace. Rupert Murdoch was trying to bring down the monarchy. The truth is that the present crop of young royals have had trouble coping with life in a global goldfish bowl. And they have been anything but discreet. Prince Charles had given full vent to his eccentric opinions on architecture, the environment and organic farming. This has invited speculation that he talks to flowers. His gawky appearance, with his jug ears and recessive Habsburg chin, even led wags to suggest that a long dead strain of congenital syphilis, perhaps inherited from the Hanoverians, had suddenly reappeared in the family, causing a morbid softening of the brain.

Despite his strange appearance and awkward manner, Prince Charles began to have girlfriends in his early twenties. He lost his virginity to Lucia Santa Cruz, the daughter of the Chilean ambassador, when he was at Cambridge. She was a graduate student, three years his senior. Later he scaled the walls of Newnham College to share a tryst with Sybilla Dorman, the daughter of the Governor General of Malta. Shortly afterwards, he escorted Audrey Buxton to the Trinity May Ball. Then, after Cambridge, Prince Charles joined the Navy where, in retaliation for his boyish pranks, he was frequently 'debagged'.

Prince Charles's position obviously attracted a lot of young ladies and the list of his girlfriends reads like an extract from Burke's Peerage: Lady Victoria Percy and her sister Lady Caroline, the daughters of the Duke of Northumberland; Lady Camilla Fane, the daughter of the Earl of Westmorland; Lady Jane Wellesley, daughter of the Duke of Wellington; Lady Henrietta Fitzroy, daughter of the Duke of Grafton; Lady Cecil Kerr, daughter of the Marquis of Lothian; the Duke of Westminster's daughter Leonora and her sister Jane, now Duchess of Roxburghe; Lady Charlotte Manners, the Duke of Rutland's daughter and her cousin Elizabeth; Lord Rupert Nevill's daughter Angela; Lord Astor's daughter Louise; Sir John Russell's daughter Georgiana; Lady 'Kanga' Tryon and the somewhat less aristocratic Sabrina Guinness of the famous stout family.

All of these liaisons took place in the glare of publicity and some of them caused problems for the Prince. When he began seeing the rich and stylish Davina Sheffield, her ex-lover, James Beard, sold the intimate details of their cohabitation to the Sunday papers. Similarly, when the Prince took up with Lord Manton's daughter Fiona Watson, a minor scandal erupted when it was discovered that she had posed in the nude for *Penthouse* magazine.

During his bachelor days, like his father before him, Prince Charles was very close to Lord Mountbatten. He would often entertain his girlfriends at Broadlands, Mountbatten's famous country home.

Then in 1972, he met the love of his life, Camilla Shand. Some say that it was the man who was to become her husband, guards officer Andrew Parker-Bowles, who first presented her to Charles at the London discotheque Annabel's. Others say that they met on the polo field. What is certain, however, is that she introduced herself to him, coyly, as the great-granddaughter of Alice Keppel – the mistress of that other famous Prince of Wales, who became Edward VII; the same Mrs Keppel who once remarked that her job was 'to curtsy first and then hop into bed'.

They established an instant rapport, sharing the same surreal and scatological sense of humour. They also shared a love of horses, fishing, hiking, the outdoors and architecture. It was with great reluctance that Charles said goodbye to her in 1973, when he was setting off to sea as an officer on HMS *Minerva*. Four weeks later, Camilla was engaged to another man. She married Andrew Parker-Bowles after a few months and, the following year, the Prince was godfather to their first child.

Charles moved on to other women, apparently undaunted. He was briefly involved with Sarah Spencer, Diana's older sister, before meeting his bride-to-be. In fact, she had nurtured a crush on Prince Andrew and had 'saved herself' for him, but she was just the type of girl the royal family were looking for: English, upper class and a virgin. This, at least, was the firm assertion of Diana's uncle, Lord Fermoy, even though she had been going out for a year with George Plumptree and, for a short time, with Prince Andrew.

While Charles and Diana were courting, the Prince also continued to date Anna Wallace – who was seeing other men – and Davina Sheffield. And, of course, he was still very close to his old friend, Camilla Parker-

Bowles. While Diana had to call her fiancé 'sir', Camilla called him 'Fred' and he called her 'Gladys'. A matter of weeks before the royal wedding, Diana discovered an expensive bracelet hidden in his desk which she thought was a wedding present for her – until she saw the initials 'F' and 'G' on it.

After a wedding watched by more than 750 million people, the couple honeymooned first at Broadlands – where Charles got up early to go fishing with Uncle Dickie – and on the Royal Yacht, where they became more passionate. Like most newly-marrieds, they went to bed early and rose late. They also took some candid pictures of each other. These, apparently, fell into the hands of the press, but no newspaper has ever dared publish them. However, the honeymoon may not have lived up to everything a romantically-inclined young girl dreams of and Diana spent much of her holiday chatting up the young sailors on the *Britannia.*

She has since flirted publicly with Mario Soares, the President of Portugal, and many others. There is no doubt that she takes a very lively interest in sex, swapping dirty jokes with Fergie and sitting in on sex therapy sessions at Relate.

Unfortunately, though, she had not always found an easy outlet for this with her husband. A year after their wedding, Prince Charles told Diana that he had absolutely no intention whatsoever of giving up his friendship with Mrs Parker-Bowles. Then, not long after the birth of Prince William in 1982, she overhead him saying on the telephone: 'Whatever happens I will go on loving you.' Obviously, these were not the sort of sentiments that a new young mother would want to hear.

The Prince and Princess of Wales, like the Queen and Prince Philip before them, quickly moved into separate bedrooms. And when, after the birth of her two healthy sons, she had fulfilled her duty to provide heirs for the throne, Diana began seeing other men. First there was Philip Dunne. She stayed out all night with him after a party and they spent a weekend together at his parents' country house when Prince Charles was away. Next, there was Major David Waterhouse, who escorted her to a David Bowie concert.

Diana has had a number of other close male friends. These include Charles's former equerry Nicholas Haslam; an upper-class hi-fi retailer, Mervyn Chaplin; and Rory Scott, whose ironing Diana did in her single days. She was also particularly close to Captain James Hewitt, who taught Prince William to ride and coaxed Diana herself back into the saddle. She corresponded with him during the Gulf War and appears to have been the cause of the break up of his long-term relationship with Emma Stewardson. The latter broke off the affair, claiming that Hewitt was besotted with Diana.

But the relationship that caused most public concern was that with James Gilbey, an upper-crust car dealer and a member of the famous gin family. They had been friends before she was married and he was, it was presumed, nothing more than a shoulder for her to cry on. But one evening in 1989, Diana was being tailed by two journalists. They watched as her private detective, Sergeant David Sharp, dropped her off at Gilbey's flat at 8.20 pm. The reporters waited outside and for the next five hours no one else entered or left.

Sergeant Sharp returned at 11 pm to pick up the Princess. However, she did not come to the door. Then, at 1 am, she eventually emerged, looked furtively up and down the street and drove off with Sergeant Sharp.

When quizzed on the matter, Gilbey said tactfully that they had been playing bridge. However, you need four people to play bridge and he had no other visitors that night.

Although the press began to speculate that something as going very wrong with the royal marriage, the Prince and Princess of Wales still made a convincing display of public togetherness. Then Andrew Morton's book *Diana, Her True Story* was published, apparently with her tacit approval. This caused a sensation, outlining as it did the misery that her marriage had become. The furore over this had scarcely died away, when Diana was catapulted into the headlines once again, as the 'Squidgygate' tapes were revealed.

Although tapes purporting to be of telephone conversations between Gilbey and the Princess of Wales on New Year's Eve 1989 and 4th January 1990 had been in circulation for some time, the British press had suppressed them. It was only when, two years later, they surfaced in the United States that editors in London decided to run them.

The tapes reveal two people who are very much in love and obviously physically intimate. They plan a forthcoming assignation. He refers to her by the pet name of 'Squidgy', while she curses 'this f . . . ing family'.

Although it would be impossible to prove that the man and woman on the tapes are Gilbey and the Princess, experts are convinced that they are authentic.

The Squidgygate tape was soon followed by another, which surfaced in Australia. This purported to be a telephone conversation between Prince Charles and

Mrs Camilla Parker-Bowles, recorded just two weeks before the 'Squidgy' phone call. In it, a man, possibly the Prince, tells his lover that he wants to be a tampon, so that he can be that intimate with her. However, he jokingly concedes that, knowing his luck, he will probably end up flushed down a toilet.

Despite one final attempt to bluff things out on their royal visit to South Korea, the Prince and Princess of Wales eventually separated. Their marriage is now at an end, raising all sorts of constitutional questions. Some senior churchmen, for example, have expressed the opinion that, because of his relationship with Mrs Parker-Bowles, Prince Charles should never be allowed to take the throne.

But Prince Charles seems determined to have his cake and eat it. In a prolonged television interview and a book, he admitted committing adultery and talked of his love for Mrs Parker-Bowles. She divorced her husband and has been seen with Charles at parties. They have even kissed publicly.

The Princess of Wales retaliated in kind. She said that she did not think her husband was fit to be king, confirmed that James Hewitt had been her lover and said that she wanted to be a roving ambassador for Britain. This was extraordinary. By admitting adultery, she was confessing treason – still a capital offence in Great Britain. Under the 13th-century treason act, which is still in force, Hewitt stands to be beheaded, while the Princess of Wales's punishment is public burning. Now what is she going to wear for the occasion? Are the Emanuels going to run up something in asbestos? How much are the global TV rights worth? I think we should be told.

Treason, one would have thought, is an extremely serious offence. And the law is very explicit on the penalties incurred by those involved in violating the consort of the heir to the throne. Strangely, though, no action has been taken against the Princess of Wales or James Hewitt. As far as one can make out, Scotland Yard do not even seem to be investigating the matter.

In the face of the authorities' impotence, the Princess of Wales is now racking up an impressive list of putative traitors. Her name has been linked with millionaire art-dealer Oliver Hoare. Their friendship ended in 1994, among allegations that she made malicious telephone calls. A married man, Hoare admitted that he was bewitched by Diana.

She met David Waterhouse, a major in the Life Guards and Gulf War veteran, in 1986. Unlike James Hewitt, Major Waterhouse has so far had the good taste to restrain himself from rushing into print. We are 'just good friends', he says.

Merchant banker Philip Dunne met Diana through his sister Millie. They became close when he joined her skiing party in Klosters in 1987, much to Charles's annoyance. Speculation peaked when they spent a weekend alone together while Prince Charles was out of the country. Prince Andrew is said to have warned him off and, in 1989, he married Domenica Fraser, daughter of the chairman of Rolls-Royce. Diana turned out for the wedding, against Charles' wishes.

Another merchant banker, William van Straubenzee, has been a companion. They have been friends since childhood and, before she was married, she used to wash his shirts.

Barry Mannakee, Diana's favourite body guard and a married man, was sacked for being 'over-familiar'. Eight months later he died in a motorbike accident, leaving her devastated.

Diana met England rugby captain Will Carling working out at the exclusive Harbour Club. They became close. In 1995, it was reported that he had a special phone line installed to take her calls and called her 'The Boss'. Speculation about their relationship took its toll on his marriage to TV presenter Julia Carling. They separated. Will Carling and Diana stopped seeing each other soon after. But she continued her keep-fit routine at the Harbour Club, where she met wealthy property developer Christopher Whalley. The press reported that they spent a weekend at his Yorkshire farmhouse and lunched together, privately, in Kensington Palace.

All this was too much for the Queen, who asked Charles and Diana to put an end to their fourteen-year marriage. Lawyers went into a huddle. As debate raged about the constitutional ramifications of all this, the Archbishop of Canterbury announced that although Charles would not be allowed to marry Camilla Parker-Bowles in an Anglican church, the Church of England would bless the union and, the Archbishop said, such an arrangement would in no way prevent Prince Charles from becoming king or titular head of the Anglican Church.

Sadly the rest of the royal family also seem to have inherited the less desirable genes of their debauched forebears. Prince Andrew's pre-marital excesses are well known. His first love was Sandi Jones, a willowy blonde whom he first met in Montreal at the age of sixteen. She attended his twenty-first birthday party and also accompanied him on a trip to the United States, where his behaviour was so loutish that he was dubbed the 'Duke of Yob' by the British press. The American media called it: 'the most unpleasant royal visit since they burned the White House in 1812'.

A rich but spoilt mother's boy who was openly contemptuous of the common people, the Duke of York tried to earn himself a reputation as a lover. One of the first to try his mettle was the former Bond girl and Miss UK contestant, Carolyn Seward, who was spotted leaving Buckingham Palace early one morning by a footman.

Andrew turned up to Princess Margaret's fiftieth birthday party accompanied by Gemma Curry, a twenty-one-year-old model, but his attention soon turned towards the thirty-two-year-old actress and dancer, Finola Hughes. She left him to go to America to appear in soap operas. Her place was soon taken by the thirty-one-year-old model Katie Rabett, who fell dramatically from royal favour when nude pictures of her were published in the tabloids. She later went on to marry the drag comedian, Kit Hesketh Harvey.

Another soap star, Catherine Oxenburg from *Dynasty*, was also linked with Prince Andrew. Then he fell for Carolyn Herbert. Carolyn seemed to be an eminently suitable match. She was the daughter of Lord Porchester, the Queen's racing manager. Once again, though, the liaison came to nothing and, just a year later, she married bloodstock agent John Warren.

Andrew's affair with the topless model Vicki Hodge was received with much less enthusiasm by the press. The couple met up when the Prince's ship, HMS *Invincible*, docked in Barbados where she had a holiday home. Hodge tried to put reporters off the scent by having him pose with her friend Tracy Lamb. This reticence did not last long, however, and Vicki took £40,000 from the Sunday papers for her explicit version of their romps.

Apparently, Vicki soon discovered why Andrew's affairs had all been so brief. With most of his girlfriends, the important things had finished far too quickly. So, in an effort to slow him down, one ex-lover had advised the Prince to count. Vicky said that what she found most disconcerting was that he counted out loud.

Thirty-seven-year-old Vicki was worldly wise and quickly took things in hand. Under the Caribbean skies, she claimed to have converted 'Randy Andy' from a sprinter into a marathon runner.

One can only hope that his next lover, Koo Stark, was suitably grateful. After her career as a soft-porn starlet, she should at least have been able to separate the wheat from the chaff. However, with her erotic exploits playing at sleazy Soho cinemas, it was felt by the Palace that she was not Duchess of York material.

Instead, they preferred Sarah Ferguson, the live-in lover of racing driver Paddy McNally. Fergie also had the support of Charles because her father, Major Ron Ferguson, was the Prince's polo manager.

Their marriage was passionate at first and their very public displays of affection sometimes embarrassed friends. On one occasion, the Prince even interrupted a naval exercise so that he could spend two hours with her in a cabin on a support ship. The excuse – seasickness.

But Fergie soon tired of 'Randy Andy', who was always away on duty. In 1990, she complained that they had only spent forty-two nights together. To make matters worse, when he was home he devoted most of his energies to playing golf.

Bored, Fergie began gallivanting round London clubs with the newly-liberated Princess Di and jetting off on endless holidays at the taxpayers' expense. She also shredded all Prince Andrew's love-letters on the pretext that they might be stolen. In the meantime, Major Ron had found himself the subject of some embarrassing photographs taken at the Wigmore Club, a London massage parlour where sexual services were also provided.

These snapshots heralded a veritable deluge of incriminating pictures, which were to haunt the royal family throughout the coming year.

In January 1992, 120 photographs were found by a cleaner in the London flat of Texan playboy Steve Wyatt. They showed the American and Fergie on holiday together, sunning themselves by the pool. Although the pictures seemed innocent enough, there was something in the complex relationship between Andrew, Fergie and Wyatt that led the Prince to ask for a divorce and to turn for succour to his former lover Koo Stark. Another old flame, thirty-eight-year-old divorcée Jane Roxburghe also provided a shoulder for him to cry on.

The Queen ordered Fergie to stop seeing Wyatt, but the newspapers reported that she secretly visited his flat in Cadogan Square on at least two more occasions.

To escape from the growing scandal, Fergie headed out to Florida where she stayed with a notorious womanizer, sixty-six-year-old Robert Forman, who prided himself on his boast of going out with girls young enough to be his granddaughters.

Then she went for a holiday in the Far East with her financial adviser Johnny Bryan, who was later dispatched back to Britain to find out what sort of divorce settlement the Duchess could expect. Unless a satisfactory figure could be arrived at, there was always the threat that the Duchess of York might publish her memoirs, which, at a conservative estimate, could be worth £4 million.

It was at this sensitive juncture that details of Major Ron's affair with a glamorous thirty-three-year-old horsewoman, Lesley Player, were serialized in the Sunday papers. To put the icing on the cake, Fergie was photographed topless in the south of France, with her children and two male bodyguards looking on. And who should be with her, kissing, cuddling, tucking her hair behind her ears, rubbing suntan lotion into her naked back and sucking her toes, but the same financial adviser who was negotiating her divorce, Johnny Bryan.

Princess Anne fared little better. She married on the rebound from her polo-playing commodity broker Sandy Harper, who broke off with her suddenly to marry model Peta Secombe. Anne married a fellow horse-riding fanatic, Captain Mark Phillips, reputedly called 'Fog' at Sandhurst because he was thick and wet.

They had two children but gradually drifted apart. Mark Phillips's name was linked with the former Miss India and high-class call-girl Pamela Bordes, whom he had met during an equestrian weekend at Gleneagles. She was invited to stay, with a friend, in a cottage on the Gatcombe Park estate while Anne was away.

Worse revelations were to follow. A forty-year-old New Zealand art teacher named Heather Tonkin lodged a paternity suit against Phillips, claiming that her six-year-old daughter 'Bunny' was the result of their one-night stand at the Auckland Hotel in 1984.

They had met, she said, at a party. Later that night he called her and asked her to drive to his hotel. Then, in a gesture that was reminiscent of the old Edwardian horse parties, he offered to leave his riding boots outside the door, so that she would be sure to find the right room.

Subsequently, regular payments were made to Ms Tonkin in her capacity as 'an equestrian consultant'. However, once the affair came out into the open, the suit was settled out of court.

The final nail in the coffin of Princess Anne's marriage came when her former bodyguard Peter Cross asked the Sunday papers for £600,000 for the story of his 'special relationship' with his employer. Then Anne's love-letters to the Queen's equerry, Commander Timothy Laurence, were stolen from his briefcase. The contents of these were never revealed but they were coyly described as 'affectionate'. Unlike her brothers', Anne's affair remained discreet until a divorce had been organized. The couple then married speedily and with a minimum of fuss. They, at least, appear to have achieved a happy ending. They separated in 2001.

As for the scandals affecting the rest of the current royal family, it is impossible to make out whether they are the product of years of in-breeding from deeply inadequate stock or whether their peccadilloes have just been magnified by the incessant glare of publicity.

The gadabout Duke of Kent's son, Prince Michael, married a Catholic divorcée, Marie-Christine von

Reibnitz, who had previously captivated Prince William of Gloucester before he was tragically killed in a plane crash. Lord Louis Mountbatten is said to have arranged the annulment of her first marriage to Tom Trowbridge, but the royal connection has not helped the Princess settle down.

According to the *News of the World*, she has spent much time since her second marriage with the Texan multi-millionaire Ward Hunt. Her name has also been linked with Elizabeth Taylor's former partner, Senator John Warner. However, the greatest scandal concerning the Princess arose when it was revealed that her father had been a high-ranking SS officer – a fact that both the government and the Palace must have known.

Princess Alexandra's daughter, Marina Ogilvy, hit the headlines when it emerged that she was living with a leather-clad freelance photographer called Paul Mowatt. The couple had a baby, although Marina told the press that her mother had urged her to have an abortion.

Later, Marina Ogilvy revealed that she had once picked up a painter and decorator, Phil Filton, in a pub and taken him back to Kensington Palace for sex. Their affair lasted just six days. Defying convention yet again, she then married Paul Mowatt without first asking for permission from the Queen, as is required by the Royal Marriages Act. The bride wore black.

Marina's antics did not end there, however, for she was soon on view in the tabloids again, this time photographed in skin-tight leather and thigh boots. Reporters went on to tell how she had attended a party in rubber clothing where, it was alleged, wild sex took place and drugs were available.

'I'm just an ordinary person trying to live my life,' she said in answer to her critics. This comment had a touch of irony about it for, unlike her fellow royals, Marina appeared to revel in the attention of the press.

Princess Margaret's son, furniture-maker David Linley gained rather less publicity when he took to wearing lipstick. Although he had several female escorts at this twenty-ninth birthday party, he preferred to dance with the drag queens from Soho's infamous Madam Jo Jo's.

Linley's younger sister, Lady Sarah Armstrong Jones, is said to have stolen her first boyfriend from Lady Helen Windsor, the daughter of the Duke and Duchess of Kent. She then fell for Cosmo Fry, a divorced man seven years her senior, but is now happily ensconced with the painter Daniel Chatto. The widow of the impresario Robin Fox maintains that Daniel Chatto is in fact the product of an illicit relationship between her former husband and Ros Chatto, who is the wife of the actor Tom Chatto. She also says that Fox had previously had an affair with Princess Marina, the mother of the current Duke of Kent.

Lady Helen Windsor is nicknamed 'Melons' because of her voluptuous breasts, which have often drawn the attention of the paparazzi. At seventeen, she was photographed dancing half naked in a London club, but she is now respectably married to art dealer Tim Taylor.

If in doubt, have a royal wedding. It is a tactic that has always worked in the past. There was only one candidate left – Prince Edward, who had been seen publicly kissing a woman, Sophie Rhys-Jones.

Prince Edward and Sophie Rhys-Jones eventually got married in 1999 – but not without the necessary amount of farce. In the run-up to the royal wedding topless photos of Sophie circulated. The great British public lapped it up and no one felt sorry for Edward. It was assumed that tits did not interest him. The music at their wedding was provided by the Band of the Royal Marines, who played "Mustang Sally", "Delilah" and, of course, the Village People's "YMCA".

But things had already got tasteless with James Hewitt publishing a 'novelised' version of his torrid love affair with Diana called *Princess in Love*, ostensibly written by Anna Pasternak, a distant relative of the author of *Dr Zhivago* and former girlfriend of Hewitt. Later he produced his own book *Love and War* and, after Diana's death, tried to sell her love letters.

Meanwhile, Kitty Kelly, the controversial author of *Jackie Oh!* and *Nancy Reagan: The Unauthorised Biography*, which tells of Nancy's afternoon session with Frank Sinatra upstairs at the White House, spilt the beans on the House of Windsor in her book *The Royals*. This revealed, for example, that George VI could not get it up and Queen Elizabeth (later the Queen Mother) had to be impregnated using a turkey baster. However, the publishers did not dare risk an accusation of treason and only published the book in the US, depriving British readers of the inside story. It can, of course, be purchased on the internet.

Even after Charles and Di separated the feud continued. Diana appeared on *Panorama* in 1995 and admitted committing adultery and begged to be our 'Queen of Hearts'. She said she wanted to be a British goodwill ambassador to the world – despite the fact that, as consort to the heir to the throne, by admitting adultery, she was also technically admitting treason. No one from Scotland Yard was sent to investigate.

Diana then threw herself into a charm offensive. She was seen very publicly doing good works. There were plenty of photo opportunities showing her with sick children. And, in front of the world's TV cameras, she began a campaign against land mines. This blew Charles off the front pages completely. She won a £15-million divorce settlement, but was forced to drop the title 'HRH' in return.

Then she shot herself in the foot by beginning an affair with Dodi Al Fayed, son of Harrods boss Mohamed Al Fayed. This was a dangerous move. Mohamed Al Fayed's business methods had long been a source of criticism and he had been refused a British passport. Although Dodi Al Fayed himself listed his profession as 'movie producer', he was better known for his activities on the casting couch than those behind the lens. The newspapers referred to him more accurately as 'millionaire playboy'.

Dodi dropped Calvin Klein model Kelly Fisher to woo Diana on his yacht on the Côte d'Azur. Their love blossomed in front of the telephoto lenses of the paparazzi for the delectation of tabloid readers worldwide. Meanwhile, Charles seized the opportunity to walk out the freshly divorced Camilla, laying on her fiftieth birthday bash. It seemed the scandal would never end. But end it did, tragically.

Mohamed Al Fayed revelled in the publicity his son's royal affair afforded him. He bought the house in Paris where the last British royals to be ousted by scandal, Edward and Mrs Simpson, had spent their exile. It was rumoured that this was where his son and the exiled Princess of Wales would set up home too.

But it was not to be. On the night of 30 August 1997,

Dodi and Di enjoyed a romantic dinner at the Ritz Hotel in Paris, where he proposed – though a Hollywood starlet was quick to say that Dodi was already engaged to her and produced a rock to prove it. The couple left the Ritz late that evening apparently on their way to view their putative matrimonial home. On the way, the car they were being driven in smashed into a pillar in an underpass, killing them both.

Criticism of Di ended that moment. Fears that the mother of the heir to the throne – and hence a future head of the Church of England – might marry a Muslim were put aside. No further mention was made of the fact that Di's marriage to Dodi Al Fayed would have been opposed by the Establishment because he was, shall we say, tinted. But the idea that the powers that be were so against the match that they had the happy couple bumped off has spawned a lively new outlet for conspiracy theorists. The book *Death of a Princess* claims that Di was pregnant and had converted to Islam before her death, while Mohamed Al Fayed says that the couple were killed by the British security services acting on the orders of the Duke of Edinburgh.

'Their relationship was a very serious matter,' he told reporters from *Time* magazine. 'Maybe a future king is going to have a half-brother who is a 'nigger', and Mohamed Al Fayed is going to be the stepgrandfather of the future king. This is how they think, this Establishment. They are a completely different type of human being.'

The Press, perhaps feeling a little guilty over their own role in the hounding of Di, now shot the line that the fairytale princess had died in the arms of her handsome young sheikh. When the royal family maintained their usual regal decorum, they were pilloried for being cold, old-fashioned and out of touch. The fresh young modernising Prime Minister Tony Blair had to step in and called her, with an innocent shrug, 'the People's Princess'. Such was the mood of the country that nobody threw up.

Nevertheless the tabloid-reading public blamed the paparazzi for hounding Di to her death. Echoing public sentiment, the press were vilified from the pulpit at Diana's funeral in Westminster Abbey by Diana's brother, the adulterous Earl Spencer, whose own messy divorce was already attracting the newpapers' scrutiny.

Slowly Prince Charles turned the situation to his advantage. With Di dead, Charles now had no rival on the global stage. He was now keeper of the flame – and the royal children. Even when Camilla emerged as stepmother-in-waiting, no one said a thing. Everything was going swimmingly.

But then, in an ill-judged move, biographer and journalist Polly Toynbee did an Andrew Morton, publishing *The Prince's Story*. The book told the story of the royal marriage from the Prince's side, seemingly with the collusion of, if not Charles himself, certainly those in his camp. When it came to the key issue – adultery – his defence was simply 'she did it first'. Suddenly, the longest-running royal scandal of the twentieth century showed that, even though its central, most glittering character had been written out, it still had legs.

Charles continues to walk out with Camilla, though the British public are singularly resistant to her charms. Her cause was not helped when, in 1999, her twenty-four-year-old son Tom Parker-Bowles admitted to using cocaine. He was a good friend of William and Harry, and had even taken William to nightclubs with him. Previously he had been arrested for carrying marijuana and ecstasy at Oxford, but the charges had been mysteriously dropped.

Harry admitted to using cannabis in 2002 and was sent to rehab by his dad, while William was kissed by Claudia Schiffer and exchanged emails with Britney Spears. At his twenty-first birthday party he was kissed by stand-up comedian Aaron Barschak who had gatecrashed Windsor Castle dressed as Osama bin Laden, and later that year he snogged an Australian model at a reception.

For well over a thousand years now the royal family have provoked feelings of amusement, outrage or plain envy by their lascivious and often faintly ridiculous sexual antics. And with the current crop of royals we are guaranteed much more of the same.

CHRONOLOGY

SAXONS AND DANES	Accession	Died
Egbert	827	839
Ethelwulf	839	858
Ethelbald	858	860
Ethelbert	858	865
Ethelred	865	871
Alfred the Great	871	899
Edward the Elder	899	924
Athelstan	924	939
Edmund	939	946
Eadred	946	955
Eadwig	955	959
Edgar	959	975
Edward the Martyr	975	978
Ethelred II ('the Unready')	978	1016
Edmund Ironside	1016	1016
Canute the Dane	1017	1035
Harold I	1035	1040
Hardicanute	1040	1042
Edward the Confessor	1042	1066
Harold II	1066	1066

NORMANS	Accession	Died
William I	1066	1087
William II	1087	1100
Henry I	1100	1135
Stephen, Count of Blois	1135	1154

PLANTAGENETS	Accession	Died
Henry II	1154	1189
Richard I	1189	1199
John	1199	1216
Henry III	1216	1272
Edward I	1272	1307
Edward II	1307	dep.1327
Edward III	1327	1377
Richard II	1377	dep.1399
Henry IV	1399	1413
Henry V } Lancaster	1413	1422
Henry VI	1422	dep.1461
Edward IV } York	1461	1483
Edward V	1483	1483
Richard III	1483	1485

TUDORS	Accession	Died
Henry VII	1485	1509
Henry VIII	1509	1547
Edward VI	1547	1553
Jane	1553	1554
Mary I	1554	1558
Elizabeth I	1558	1603

STUARTS	Accession	Died
James I (VI of Scotland)	1603	1625
Charles I	1625	beh.1649

COMMONWEALTH DECLARED, 19 MAY 16

STUARTS (Restoration)	Accession	Died
Charles II	1660	1685
James II (VII of Scotland)	1685	dep.1688

Interregnum 11 Dec. 1688 to 13 Feb. 1689

	Accession	Died
William III and Mary II	1689	1702
		1694
Anne	1702	1714

HOUSE OF HANOVER	Accession	Died
George I	1714	1727
George II	1727	1760
George III	1760	1820
George IV	1820	1830
William IV	1830	1837
Victoria	1837	1901

HOUSE OF SAXE-COBURG	Accession	Died
Edward VII	1901	1910

HOUSE OF WINDSOR	Accession	Died
George V	1910	1936
Edward VIII	1936	Abd. 1936
George VI	1936	1952
Elizabeth II	1952	

INDEX

243

INDEX

244

INDEX

INDEX

INDEX

INDEX

INDEX